CONNECTIONS
WORKBOOK

JILL S. LEVENSON & JOHN W. MORIN

CONNECTIONS WORKBOOK

Sage Publications, Inc.
International Educational and Professional Publisher
Thousand Oaks ▪ London ▪ New Delhi

For information:

Sage Publications, Inc.
2455 Teller Road
Thousand Oaks, California 91320
E-mail: order@sagepub.com

Sage Publications Ltd.
6 Bonhill Street
London EC2A 4PU
United Kingdom

Sage Publications India Pvt. Ltd.
M-32 Market
Greater Kailash I
New Delhi 110 048 India

Printed in the United States of America

ISBN 0-7619-2193-1

06 07 7 6 5 4 3 2

Acquiring Editor:	Nancy Hale
Editorial Assistant:	Heather Gotlieb
Production Editor:	Diane S. Foster
Editorial Assistant:	Candice Crosetti
Typesetter:	Danielle Dillahunt
Cover Designer:	Michelle Lee

Contents

Acknowledgments

The *Connections Workbook* is the culmination of years of shaping our work with sexually abusive families into a structured format. As we watched families struggle to change, so did our ideas, theories, and practices. Working daily with the complexities of sexual deviance rarely has brought us to firm conclusions but has always expanded our ways of thinking about the dynamics of sexual violence within families. In this, the first Sage edition of the *Connections Workbook*, we have added a significant amount of new material to the version we self-published several years ago.

This workbook has been inspired by the courage it takes families to survive the trauma of child sexual abuse. It would not have been possible without the contributions of the men, women, and children we've worked with, who bravely faced their problems and shared with us their stories, their pain, their fears, and their hopes. Of course, all names and identifying information have been changed to protect the confidentiality of our clients.

Special thanks to Cory Jewell and Steve Jensen for allowing us to borrow the "journey" created by their mothers in treatment and for their review, support, and encouragement of this project. Thanks also to Cindy Lawlor for her review, suggestions, and reminders about the victim's point of view. We have watched Denise Hunter, our associate, make *Connections* come alive as she has empowered clients to make profound and sometimes unexpected changes in the interests of family healing and child safety. We thank David Wood for believing in our work and encouraging us to pursue professional publication, Terry Hendrix for helping to make it happen, and Nancy Hale for her support as our editor.

We hope the *Connections* program makes a difference for victims of sexual assault, who need their families to come to their rescue.

This project is dedicated to Stephanie, Merissa, Rachel, Chloe, and Adam, who remind us every day how precious childhood truly is.

CHAPTER
1
Common Feelings of Parents and Partners

Welcome to the *Connections* program. We're glad you're here, but let's be honest: You're probably not. Most people start out at *Connections* wishing they could be anywhere else. That's only natural. They don't know what to expect, and they're afraid they might be misunderstood or judged. They know they will be expected to talk about things that are deeply disturbing, and that may be the last thing they want to do. Most of all, they just wish the sexual abuse that brought them here had never happened.

If you're like many nonoffending parents, you have probably suffered in silence since you found out about the sexual abuse. You may feel as though you have no one to talk to, and you may be convinced that no one can understand how you feel. And you may be right! People who have never experienced sexual abuse in their families have no idea how devastating it can be.

You may feel that you don't need to be involved in this program—after all, it was someone else who committed the abuse. You were probably asked to come here by your social worker, the court, or by your partner. If this program is part of a court order, you may feel that you are being punished. But the *Connections* program is not punishment. It is an opportunity for you to learn more about sexual abuse, your child, your partner, yourself, and about creating a safe home for your family.

You might notice that in this book the pronoun *he* is used to refer to sexual abusers, and *she* is used to refer to you, the nonoffending parent. Although female child abusers do exist (and possibly are more common than we think), the majority of abusers referred to the authorities are men, and the overwhelming majority of individuals referred to programs like *Connections* are women. Likewise, the pronoun *she* is usually used in this book to refer to the victim, although boys are also victimized by sexual abuse in the home. Please forgive these simplifications we've made for the sake of readability.

What Is Child Sexual Abuse?

Child sexual abuse includes any sexual touching, fondling, oral-genital contact, or rape of a child by an adult. For an adult to expose their genitals in a sexual way or to "peep" at an undressed child in a sexual way is also abuse. For an adult to talk sexually to a child may constitute abuse if the adult is using the child for his own sexual arousal. *Any* kind of sexual activity between an adult and a child under 18 is child abuse. A child may be abused by a parent, relative caretaker, older child, trusted adult friend, teacher, babysitter, youth leader, neighbor, or stranger.

Child sexual abuse is never the child's fault. Even when a child acts in a way that seems sexually provocative to an adult, it is always the adult's responsibility to set limits and teach right from wrong. Even so-called "consensual" sexual activity involving children is abuse. We say "so-called" because the truth is that children (even teenagers) cannot consent to sex, because they do not truly understand the implications or consequences of their decisions. You cannot consent to something you do not fully understand.

Child sexual abuse is not only about sex. Sexual abuse is about taking advantage of a child's innocence, trust, and desire to please. The abuse is not simply in the sexual activity but in the *betrayal:* The more powerful adult exploits the child's trust for his own selfish, hurtful purpose. It is this betrayal of trust that is often most damaging to child victims.

Child sexual abuse ranges from unwanted kissing, exposure, peeping, touching, or fondling to oral sex, penetration, or sodomy. Although some of these behaviors seem worse than others, it is important to remember that to the child, abuse is abuse. You might say, "at least she wasn't penetrated," or "it was only fondling," or "he only touched her breast." It is adults who think of sex as related primarily to intercourse, that kissing or fondling is not "sex." To the child, the real abuse is not the physical touching but *what it means.* It is the manipulation and deceit, the stealing of innocence, the betrayal of the soul that is most damaging.

You will learn later about the many ways in which sexual abuse can change a child's life and leave long-lasting emotional damage.

Why Should I Learn About Child Sexual Abuse?

Because your child needs you to. Children need adults to understand their feelings, to respond to them when they are hurting, and to keep them safe from harm. If your child has been sexually abused, that child needs you to understand how the abuse has affected his or her life. Your willingness to educate yourself about sexual abuse is a gift to your child—and an essential part of your child's healing.

Your child needs you to understand how to keep him or her safe. You might believe that your partner will never abuse again. You hope, of course, that he won't. But if you rule out the possibility that it could happen, you are actually increasing the risk for your child. If you don't believe abuse could happen, you won't take precautions to prevent it from happening. If you are living with (or plan to live with) a sexual abuser, your commitment to understanding and minimizing the risk in your home is crucial for your child's safety.

My Child Was Sexually Abused by My Partner

When you found out that your partner was being accused of sexually abusing your child, your life changed forever. Most likely, a social worker or police officer knocked on your door, and suddenly everything in your world was turned upside down. The disclosure of sexual abuse creates a crisis of confusion, fear, and overwhelming pain.

At first, you were probably in shock. You couldn't believe what was happening. The allegation was probably totally unexpected. You might have thought at first that your child was mistaken or misunderstood or that the social workers or police had blown things out of proportion. This is a common and understandable reaction. We all react to unexpected happenings with disbelief, especially when they are so painful. Many women report going through the first days or weeks following the disclosure in a daze.

Then, before you even had a chance to get over the initial shock, you may have had more shocks to deal with. If your partner was arrested, you may have had to locate a lawyer, borrow money for bail, or even go to court. These experiences are often humiliating and intimidating. Maybe your children were removed from your home by the state and put into emergency foster care.

Suddenly, everything that was important to you was gone! And no one seemed to be explaining anything to you. Some people seemed to be blaming you. You may have felt that you were being asked to make life-changing decisions without having a chance to think about them. For instance, a social worker might have made you feel you had to choose immediately between your husband and your children or face dire consequences. You might have felt that you were being forced to abandon your husband. You didn't understand your rights. You had no time to plan for the future. Mostly, you were bewildered and terribly hurt.

Later, you probably found that you were extremely angry at your partner. Even if you have decided to stay together and try to work things out, you may find that you continue to be resentful toward him. You may wonder if you can ever trust him again. You might feel that you are trapped in an unhappy marriage and wonder if you can ever rebuild it. Most couples find that even when they are committed to staying together and working through their problems, at times it seems impossible. The truth is that a sacred trust was betrayed when your partner abused your child. For most couples, working through all of the anger and resentment will be a long, painful road. Eventually, for some couples, acceptance can lead to a new beginning. Other couples will decide that the relationship cannot be rebuilt after all.

Most people have an imaginary line that they draw in their minds. You may have heard women say, for example, "If my husband ever cheated on me, I'd leave him," or "If my husband ever beat me, I'd kick him out." Chances are, if someone had ever asked you, "What would you do if your partner molested your child," your response would have been immediate: "I'd kill him!"

But, suddenly, when confronted with a real accusation of sexual abuse, your previous assumptions have gone out the window. The only way some women can cope with the allegations is to deny them. It may just be too painful to accept that your partner could sexually abuse your child. You convince yourself there must be some kind of mistake. You might even accuse your child of lying. If you felt forced to make decisions about your marriage right away, you might have denied the abuse partly to avoid making these painful decisions.

And so you are left not knowing what to believe, feeling torn between your partner and your child, and overwhelmed by the wrenching changes in your life. Whichever way you turn, there is no way out. If you believe your child, you betray your partner. If you believe your partner, you betray your child. *Suddenly, you have to choose between two of the people you love most in the world, and it hurts.* You are afraid of losing them both.

And nobody seems to realize this! While you are facing your partner's incarceration, the loss of his income, the loss of your relationship, and your painful feelings about the abuse, some people may be accusing you of not protecting your child. They say that you should have known, should have seen, should have prevented it, should have stopped it. They may say you are choosing your partner over the children. You may feel guilty and wonder if you *are* to blame!

Connections is about making sense of what has happened and understanding the options and choices that lie ahead. *Connections* is about making informed, educated decisions. For families that want to stay together, *Connections* is about learning how that can be done more *safely*.

My Partner Abused Somebody Else's Child

If your partner abused someone else's child, you may not have dealt with the conflicting feelings some mothers have. You may not have had immediate concerns about your children's safety, but you still may have had to deal with the consequences of your partner's crime. You probably felt angry, betrayed, and confused. You might have suddenly felt like you were living with a stranger. And, after thinking about it, you might have wondered if he would do something to your own children as well.

Maybe you didn't know your partner at the time of his offense. Maybe you are in a relationship with him now and he told you about his past. You want to believe that his abusive behavior is all behind him, but a little part of you may wonder how well you really know him.

If your partner abused someone else's children and he is living (or planning to live) with you and your children, it is essential for you to understand what led up to his offenses, what his offense patterns are, and what his prevention plan consists of, so you can protect your own children from potential abuse.

But My Partner Said He Didn't Do It

Almost all sexual offenders deny their crimes. Who can blame them? They are afraid of the obvious consequences—going to prison and losing everything. It is human nature to want to avoid punishment, and sex offenders are no different from anyone in that regard. What makes them different is the depth and intensity of their denial. After all, they have a lot to lose.

But most sexual offenders also feel ashamed of their actions. They don't want to admit what they did because they are afraid of losing you. They know that if you believe the accusations, you might want a divorce, might take the children away, might even testify against them. You might hate them. The shame and guilt they feel makes it enormously difficult for them to admit to what they've done. In fact, if your partner admitted to the abuse right away, he is very unusual. It might show that he is brave enough to face up to his problem.

Some sex offenders in treatment say they wanted to stop abusing their victim(s), but they couldn't ask for help. The truth is that although offenders need special treatment to learn to control their behavior, they can't seek that treatment without facing great risks. Because of mandatory child abuse reporting laws (designed to prevent ongoing abuse), if a child sex abuser goes to a therapist for help, the therapist must report the abuse to the child protection agency. The child protection agency then informs the police, and the case is investigated. Because the offender admitted to the therapist that he abused a child, his confession may be used as evidence to convict him and possibly to terminate his parental rights.

So most sex offenders deny their abusive behavior—*and they do it very convincingly.* They are practiced at it, after all. The typical offender has been denying his crimes to others (and maybe to himself) for a long time. The typical child molester has at least several, and maybe many, other victims. While the recent abuse was occurring, throughout the investigation, during the court proceedings, in prison, and maybe even in treatment, the offender continues to deny his crimes because denial has always protected him from punishment, from shame, and from the scorn of others.

Unfortunately, while the offender is busy denying his crime and protecting himself, the victim is left unsupported, afraid, and alone. Victims might be accused of lying and might feel they can't depend on adults to help. They lose trust in the very people they must depend on—their parents. And you are left wondering . . . because as much as you want to believe he didn't do it, you're not really sure. In the *Connections* program, you are going to come face to face with harsh reality. Be prepared for new surprises and new hurts.

I Hate Him—But I Still Love Him

At a time like this, it's almost too painful to admit. But you wouldn't be here if you didn't still love him. And that's really not so surprising. Until this happened, he was the man in your life—and he still is. You may not be sure that you'll get over this terrible shock or that you'll stay with him. But a part of you wants to. A part of you hopes that somehow this can be dealt with, and that things can be good again.

When other people (including some members of your own family) are questioning your judgment and pressuring you to give up on him, it's important to clarify what you're doing and why. You can start by recognizing that he's still the same person that you fell in love with, and he has the same traits that attracted you to him. Only now, he's much more complicated. You may find yourself wondering if you really do know him. He has a problem—a very serious problem, to be sure, and one you didn't know about before. But do we usually run out the door on everything we have cared about because we encounter a problem—even a very serious one?

The truth is that good people can have bad problems. It used to be that people with drinking problems were seen as nothing but "lushes." Nowadays, everyone knows that lots of alcoholics and drug addicts get the help they need and change. And once they get their problem under control, guess what? They become our friends and neighbors and coworkers—and partners—and the problem they've struggled with doesn't have to interfere in our relationships with them. We know there's a lot more to them than just their addiction.

Of course, sex offending is much more serious and more damaging to others than drinking or drugging. But everyone with a will to change can change, and there is always much more to a person than just his problem. Your partner is not just his problem. He is your lover, your friend, a hard worker, the person who makes you laugh, the father of your children—*and* he has a problem. Right now, he's hoping you will remember those other things.

You're going to find that this workbook is full of warnings: He might fool you, he might lie to you, he might reoffend, he's going to still be attracted to children. It's all true. And it's even worse than that: Some child molesters are true "pedophiles," which means their primary sexual attraction is toward children. Such men will always be dangerous and should never be allowed to be around children. These men may be extremely difficult to detect because their entire lifestyle is designed to project a false front. They may appear to be sensible, concerned, and perfectly normal. They can talk apparently sincerely about the harm sexual abuse causes and the importance of treatment. There is no way for you to be certain that your partner is not one of these men. However, you can gain some assurance by having him assessed by a knowledgeable specialist in sex offender evaluation. (The primary source of information on sex offender specialists is the Association for the Treatment of Sexual Abusers [ATSA], www.atsa.com). The sex offender evaluation should always include a review of records (including criminal and child protective service records) and polygraphing. Your *Connections* therapist might also require your partner to be polygraphed.

It is necessary for you to take all the warnings seriously because of the great harm that child sexual abuse causes. But if your partner is not a true pedophile and if he makes a real commitment to treatment, if he sticks with his plan to prevent future abuse, if he takes responsibility for controlling his behavior—with your help and understanding—then, maybe things can be safer. Different, but safer. You will always need to be aware of the potential for abuse caused by your partner's weakness. But loving anyone involves understanding their weaknesses, doesn't it?

We who treat sex offenders know them well. And guess what? Mostly, they're men with the same basic needs as anyone. They don't know how to meet their needs in a healthy way. Most of them are horribly ashamed of what they have done. No one could hate them more than they hate themselves for having this problem.

In the end, you cannot let anyone else decide what's best for you. Make your decisions with your eyes open, but base them on what you feel. And don't be ashamed to be honest about your feelings. If you still love him, tell him, and tell your family and friends. Let them know you need their support to get through this crisis, just as he needs yours.

But What About Me?

You probably have a lot of mixed feelings about this whole thing. Since the disclosure, you have probably felt a bewildering array of feelings: anger, betrayal, fear, rejection, loss of control, guilt, shame, and sadness. You might also feel depressed, anxious, lonely, and numb. You might be in denial. You might even feel some jealousy toward the victim. You might hate the child welfare workers. At times, you hate your partner; at other times, you might find yourself hating the victim. Most of all, you are very confused.

Many Nonoffending Parents Feel . . .

Anger

Whether or not your partner admits to the allegations, you probably feel angry at him. You might doubt his denial and know that he did do something inappropriate. If you know he really did commit the crime, you certainly have a right to be angry about all the losses you have suffered. At the same time, you might be angry at the victim. You may feel he or she should have told you before telling someone else. Or you may feel that somehow the victim provoked the abuse. Even if you know it wasn't the victim's fault, you may still feel resentful about the abuse and focus this anger on the victim. At times, you have probably been angry at family and friends for not understanding and at the legal system for intruding in your life.

You might be angry at yourself—for not seeing the signs, for not noticing what was happening, for not protecting your child. Most mothers feel angry at themselves, as well as guilty and ashamed, for not being able to protect their child. Remember, you did nothing to cause the abuse. Committing a sex offense is always the choice of the offender alone and is his responsibility alone. But you may realize, as you go through this book, that you ignored the signs of abuse or even chose not to believe your child when he or she tried to tell you what was happening.

Sadness

Because sexual abuse in a family results in painful losses—relationship, emotional, and financial losses—the sadness can be powerful.

Hurt

Most women report feeling hurt by their partner's sexually abusive behavior. They are wounded both by the sexual betrayal and by the partner's callous indifference toward harming the children and family. Some women will be hurt by the way their family and friends respond, rejecting and socially ostracizing their family. Crying is normal behavior at this difficult time.

Loneliness

Many women feel isolated and lonely as they learn how hard it is for others to understand their situation. It isn't easy to talk about sexual abuse, and you may feel you are dealing with it all by yourself.

> "My family doesn't talk to me anymore. They don't understand how I can stay married to my husband. We spend holidays alone, they say mean things behind my back, and I have no one to help me."

Numbness

Some women report that in the days and weeks following the disclosure, they just "go through life like a robot." Sometimes, avoiding painful feelings seems the only way to survive.

Rejection

Some women wonder "what's wrong with me? Why did my husband turn to a child?" You might feel that you aren't lovable or sexually desirable. Here is yet another way you can blame yourself, when the truth is that nothing you did caused your partner's behavior.

Betrayal

You probably felt betrayed by your partner, as if he were having an affair. Knowing your partner was sexual with someone else, especially a child, really damages the trust between you. You may also feel like you don't know your partner anymore—that he has betrayed you by hiding something from you, lying to you, turning out to be someone you didn't expect.

> "I used to put my husband on a pedestal . . . he was a hard worker and a good father. I looked up to him. Then he molested my niece, and suddenly I felt like I was married to a stranger. Suddenly, our relationship and my whole life seemed like a lie."

Fear

Most partners of abusers are afraid of many things: the outcome of the criminal case and the social services investigation, the financial hardships, the effects of the abuse on their children, the possibility that their children will be abused again. In the beginning, everything is frightening: You've never been through anything like this, and you don't know what to expect.

Loss of Control

Following a disclosure of sexual abuse, everything seems to spin out of control. The world as you've known it is forever changed. You might feel that you can't trust anyone. You might feel you can't predict what the future will bring. You might feel helpless in dealing with the legal system, helpless to communicate with your partner, or helpless to protect your children.

Guilt

Many women feel guilty about their child's abuse—that they should have known what was happening and done something to prevent it. You might feel you've failed to protect your children.

Shame

Some women describe a sense of shame. Partly, this might have to do with feeling that you failed to protect your child from harm. Partly, it stems from loving someone (your partner) who others see as a bad person. You might feel that your partner's abusive behavior is somehow a reflection on you as a mother, wife, or woman.

Embarrassment

What does it mean that you love a man who sexually abused a child? You might feel this means something is wrong with your ability to judge people or choose a mate. It is very hard to accept that someone you love did bad things. Furthermore, many states now have "public notification" laws that allow authorities to tell your neighbors that a sex offender lives in the community. You might be dealing with the shame and humiliation of having your family problems publicly aired.

You might feel that you can protect your child yourself, without help from outside agencies or therapists. You might know that your child was abused but deny it to others to protect your family and avoid legal consequences. You might be convinced that if all the authorities would just get out of your life, you could handle the problem yourself. The truth is that the problem is the *offender's,* and without the proper help, you cannot protect your child. You cannot control the offender's behavior no matter how hard you try.

Sheri was sexually abused by her father from age 4 on. As an adult, she struggled to hold onto a job, used drugs, and couldn't provide a stable environment for her 10-year-old daughter. So her daughter was being raised by her parents. Because she was afraid that her father might abuse her child, she continued to have sex with him, believing that this would keep him from touching the girl. She later found out that all along, her father was abusing her daughter as well.

Jealousy

Some mothers are horrified to find themselves jealous of their own child. When your husband made your child his romantic partner, he created a rival for his love and attention.

Depression

Depression is not just sadness. Depression is a numbing of feelings that can result from overwhelming loss. Depression can take over your body and interfere with your ability to function in your daily responsibilities. If depression leaves you unable to eat, sleep, work, or care for your children, or if you find yourself sleeping more than usual, overeating, or feeling withdrawn and without any energy, you may want to see a knowledgeable psychotherapist for individual therapy or a psychiatrist. A psychiatrist is a physician who can determine if antidepressant medication would be helpful for you.

Anxiety

Anxiety is not just about feeling a little worried or nervous. Like depression, clinical anxiety can take over your life and leave you feeling unable to function. If you are suffering from repetitive thoughts that you can't get out of your mind or if you find yourself unable to concentrate because of your troubles, a psychiatric exam might be helpful in determining if anti-anxiety medication can help you through this crisis.

Family and Friends Don't Seem to Understand

Family and friends are going through a crisis, too. Of course, you need them during this time more than they need you. But you might find that others can't give you what you need because they are too caught up in their own shock and confusion.

Your family might be angry at you for staying with the abuser. They might refuse to help you or even shut you out of their lives. Maybe they say bad things about your partner, which only adds to your hurt and confusion because you still love him. They might think they know what's best for you and tell you what to do. Or on the other hand, they might minimize the abuse, saying, "it wasn't really that big a deal."

Your partner's family might blame you for deserting him. They might blame your child for telling. Because they love your partner, it may be impossible for them to accept what he has done. Their denial of his offense may be rock hard, resistant to all reason and all evidence. Their denial might lead to their rejection of you because you believe the child.

Family and friends might not want to be around you or be around your partner. They might be afraid the abuser will molest their children. They might feel disgust or scorn about his behavior. They might simply not know what to say. It might be just too hard for your family and friends to see past the facts of the case to all the conflicting feelings you have.

The aftermath of sexual abuse is a lonely time for most nonoffending parents. If you believe your child, you will be dealing with the possibility of losing your relationship with your partner. If you deny your partner's crimes, you will not be protecting your child and might irreparably damage your relationship with your child, and you could even lose custody or your parental rights. You don't know if you can rely on the support of family and friends. Whatever you do you will probably feel that you've lost a lot—and you're right.

The Legal System

Dealing with the court system can be a frightening process. If you were in a relationship with your partner at the time of his offense, chances are good that you have been involved with the criminal justice system or the child welfare system or both. Criminal proceedings include the police investigation and the prosecution and trial (or plea bargain) of your partner's crime. Dependency (or juvenile) proceedings involve the child protective services investigation and case plan if it is determined that your child is in need of protection by the state.

If your partner was charged with a crime, you and your child might have been asked to give testimony about the abuse. This can be intimidating for both you and the child. If you believe the abuse occurred, a part of you wants to help the victim by acknowledging the crime and its consequences. The dilemma for you is that in this process you might feel you are betraying your partner and could be contributing to his conviction.

If child protective services took your case to family court, they might have asked your partner to leave the home. They may have visited your home to check on your children. They might have even placed your child in foster care and insisted that you, your partner, or your child—or all of you—enter counseling. This type of attention usually feels intrusive, and many partners feel it's unfair. You might have been accused of failing to protect your child, and in some cases, the court might be seeking to terminate your parental rights.

It might seem that no matter what you do, you can't win. If you deny the abuse, you will be seen as nonprotective. If you want to stay with your partner and work through the problems, you might be seen as being disloyal to your child. The problem is that your loyalty to your partner and your loyalty to your child seem to conflict with each other. It probably seems that there can be no happy ending for you.

Legal proceedings are emotionally and financially draining. You might have had to spend your life savings or go into debt for your partner's criminal defense or to hire an attorney to represent you in family court. You might feel that the social service agency case plan will be impossible to accomplish. You might feel that the legal system has total control over your life.

Even after the court proceedings are over, you might still be dealing with the legal system. Maybe your partner is on probation and has many court-ordered restrictions imposed on him. Protective services workers might come to your home unannounced to visit your child and might require you to attend counseling programs. It may feel like the intrusions into your life will never end.

The best thing you can do is to cooperate as well as you can with any requests or orders from a probation officer, social worker, or judge. The court orders, as unfair as they might seem at times, are intended to help families by protecting children. Although you might feel that you are being punished for your partner's behavior, take advantage of any opportunities for help that are offered.

What Many Nonoffending Parents Need After Disclosure

Many nonoffending parents or partners of sexual abusers mention common needs they had following the disclosure of sexual abuse. You probably wanted someone to talk to, you wanted to be treated with respect, and you wanted to understand what your options are regarding custody, marriage, divorce, and finances. If you were sexually victimized yourself as a child, you might have remembered your own abuse after learning about the current incident, and these memories might be painful and confusing. Of course, you want to know what has really happened to your child and what your partner really did, especially if he denies or minimizes the abuse.

You might feel like you are the only one this has happened to. You want to be reassured that your feelings are normal and that the future will hold better days. You need to know how the abuse will affect your child. You need to believe that you will never have to go through this again.

All of these things are what *Connections* is about. By talking with other parents who have had similar experiences and therapists who are experienced in dealing with sexual abuse, you will have a chance to explore all these issues and get some answers to your questions. You might also find some understanding, some sense of control, and some peace of mind.

But I Know He Won't Do It Again,
so I Don't Have to Worry

The truth is that you don't know that he won't do it again, and neither does he. He may want desperately to believe he'll never do it again. He might swear he won't do it again, and he might believe it. But unless he learns *how* not to do it again, by figuring out what happened in the first place and learning how to change his thoughts and his behavior, it could well happen again.

He might say he's learned his lesson, that he doesn't want to go to prison, that he doesn't want to hurt another child, or that he doesn't have "those feelings" anymore. He might say it was an isolated incident and that he doesn't need treatment. He might focus blame on his drinking or drug use, on the child, on you, or on the legal system. But the truth is that he knew it was wrong before he did it, he knew he could go to prison for it, he knew he was hurting the child, and he knew he could have chosen not to act on "those feelings." But he did it anyway. And if he doesn't believe it can happen again, the risk is greater that it will, because he won't be taking steps to prevent it. If *you* believe it won't happen again, the risk will also be greater, because you won't be taking steps to protect your children.

The question of whether children should ever be allowed to live in homes with known sexual abusers is a troubling one and is not to be taken lightly. The actual range of an offender's abusive behavior is truly known only to the extent that the offender admits his thoughts and actions honestly to his therapist. So realistic safety precautions are critical. Any child living with a known sexual abuser, especially one who has not yet successfully completed a *qualified* sex offender treatment program, should be considered at risk for sexual abuse.

What You Can Do

The goal of the *Connections* program is not specifically reunification. The goal is education about sexual abuse to help partners make informed and responsible choices about the safety of their children. Some women may know from the beginning that they do not want to stay with their offender partner. Other women may wish they could stay with their partner but come to learn that to do so will put the children at too great a risk of future sexual abuse. When families do choose to stay together, the nonoffending parent must fully understand the offender's sexual abuse history and his potential for reoffense. You must be able to describe the molester's offense patterns and his "grooming" behaviors so that you are prepared to recognize them in the future. You must believe without a doubt that *the potential for reoffense does exist.*

Mothers who have successfully completed *Connections* will be able to identify different types of denial. They will recognize denial in themselves and others and will understand the power of denial: how denial has compromised the safety of their children in the past and how it will compromise the safety of their children in the future if they do not learn to resist it.

In Connections, you will learn to identify the behavioral, physical, and emotional indicators of sexual abuse in children. You must know what symptoms to look for so that you do not ignore potential warning signs that your children are being abused. In addition, you will understand better how to manage the emotional and behavioral problems that children often exhibit following sexual abuse.

The protective nonoffending parent encourages open communication in the household. She does not allow her children to become isolated but instead helps them develop and maintain relationships with trusted adults. She models healthy sexual boundaries and teaches her children about appropriate touching. She reinforces the child's right to say no, to be assertive, and to ask for help.

You will develop a clear understanding of the many ways in which sexual abuse affects children. You will learn techniques for reducing shame and guilt in children and for responding to your children's special needs. The nonoffending parent of a sexually abused child must be able to support the child in her recovery. To help your victimized child, you must unequivocally believe that the sexual abuse occurred and that the offending adult, *not* the child, was responsible for this abuse.

If you are considering family reunification, your *Connections* therapist will then assist you and your partner to develop a realistic family safety plan, which includes both prevention and intervention strategies. The prevention part involves developing a list of household rules (the "safety plan") that the family will live by to promote healthy sexual boundaries and minimize the possibility of new sex abuse. Intervention strategies describe the steps a nonoffending parent will take to separate her child from the offender in the event that further child sexual abuse occurs anyway or seems likely to occur. The philosophy of *Connections* is that families who choose to stay together must *plan* to do so safely.

You love both your partner and your children. Although this program may be difficult and painful at times, you are showing your love for your family by attending. You can learn to protect your children from abuse, and you can learn to help your partner stop himself from abusing again. Although the ultimate responsibility for preventing reoffense lies solely with the perpetrator, the entire family must become invested in creating a safer home environment. After the family has developed its safety plan, each adult in the home must be willing to follow the plan and to do whatever else may be necessary to block further child sexual abuse. Your involvement in developing and following the safety plan is crucial to your child's protection from potential harm.

The Journey Through Emotional Reactions to Child Sexual Abuse
as seen through the eyes of a mother's support group

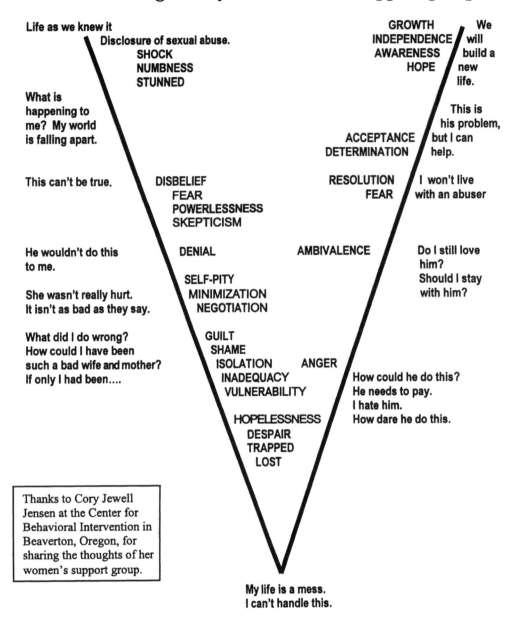

Figure 1.1. The Journey Through Emotional Reactions to Child Sexual Abuse (as seen through the eyes of a mothers' support group)

Thanks to Cory Jewell Jensen at the Center for Behavioral Intervention in Beaverton, Oregon, for sharing the thoughts of her women's support group.

At the back of this workbook, there is an attendance checklist where your *Connections* therapist will keep track of your attendance and a safety checklist to be filled out by your *Connections* therapist at the end of the program.

Figure 1.1 shows the emotional journey that many families make in coming to terms with child sexual abuse.

WORK SHEET # 1: MY FEELINGS

Name and discuss at least five (5) feelings you have about being in this program. Also, list three (3) goals you have for attending this program.

_____

_____

_____

_____

_____

_____

_____

_____

_____

_____

_____

_____

_____

Name and discuss at least six (6) feelings you had in the days, weeks, and months after you learned that your child was sexually abused or since you learned that your partner had committed a sexual offense.

_____

_____

_____

_____

_____

_____

_____

_____

_____

_____

_____

_____

Name and discuss at least six (6) things you might have needed from family,
friends, law enforcement, or child protection agencies during your crisis. What
are some of the things you still need?

_____

_____

_____

_____

_____

_____

_____

_____

_____

_____

_____

_____

_____

Name and discuss your feelings about your partner, your child, or your
partner's victim.

_____

_____

_____

_____

_____

_____

_____

_____

_____

_____

_____

_____

_____

CHAPTER 2

Denial in Family Members

What is *denial?* Denial is a defense mechanism, which means that it is a way of protecting yourself from something that is difficult to accept. We all use defense mechanisms to keep away painful feelings and to avoid situations that cause us anxiety or make us uneasy. We make excuses to convince ourselves that we are right. We ignore problems that are confusing or difficult, hoping they will magically go away. When we use denial as a defense mechanism, we are trying to avoid seeing the reality that is usually obvious to others. Denial is our way of fooling ourselves when the truth is too painful, too embarrassing, or too threatening to accept.

It may be that when you first heard about your child's abuse or your partner's offense, you thought (and said), "It can't be true!" Even when the facts seemed indisputable, you held on to the hope that somehow it would all go away. By denying the problem, you were hoping to avoid dealing with the awful feelings and the painful changes you knew you'd have to make if the accusations were true. Denial at this stage is only natural. It takes time to accept the realities of sexual abuse.

If you have since accepted that the abuse did occur, you have made it over the most difficult hurdle. But it is important to understand that denial doesn't end with simply admitting the bare facts of the abuse. There are other types of denial that will probably enter your mind and will be most tempting. Different people experience these types of denial in different ways. Denial in any form is always difficult for the denier to recognize. Even now, there is probably some denial going on in your family—and in you. It takes a strong person to see his or her own denial and face difficult truths. But the more quickly you are able to accept the problem fully and give up all forms of denial, the more you can benefit from this program and the more you can help your children and your partner.

The first and most obvious type of denial, of course, is when someone simply denies the facts of the case. This occurs when you tell yourself and others that a sexual offense did not occur. You might have continued to deny the facts even after you knew otherwise to defend your partner against criminal charges or to defend yourself in a child welfare investigation. Now, you might still be denying the facts to avoid confronting the abuse in this program. But the truth is that now, for the first time, you have more to gain by admitting the abuse happened than by denying it. Talking about the sexual abuse in therapy will not be used against you. But *not* talking will keep you locked in a secret prison of your own making.

You may feel that the police and child protective services workers have jumped to conclusions and that the evidence is not convincing. We cannot know the facts of your partner's case, of course, and there is always the possibility that your partner really is innocent and you have been sent to this program needlessly. In this book, we cannot go into the details of the complicated processes used by investigators and sex offender specialists to evaluate evidence and come to conclusions. We can only make a few observations that may help you to accept the findings of the authorities. First: Neither the police nor the child protective workers have anything to gain by twisting a child's words to find abuse where none has occurred. Second: Children rarely make up stories about being sexually abused. Third: It is extremely difficult to "coach" a child to tell a false story of being sexually abused that is convincing to professional investigators. Most important, know that your own powerful hopes and fears can make it very difficult for you to see the evidence objectively. If your real reason for insisting that your partner is innocent is that "you just know he's not that kind of person," or that he seems so *sincere* when he tells you he didn't do it, you owe it to yourself to read this book carefully and do the exercises in it. You owe it to your children to have the courage to put your feelings aside and open your mind to rationally explore all possible explanations for the evidence.

Sexual abuse occurs and thrives in secrecy. Letting go of secrets is often the first step toward ending the abuse. Most nonoffending parents feel embarrassed and ashamed to talk about their partner's behavior and their child's abuse, which is why they keep it a secret. Now, you have the opportunity to share your secret with others who will understand you and not judge you, because they know what it is like to have shameful secrets of their own. The bottom line is that nothing good can come from counseling while you are denying the fact that sexual abuse took place. You will be left feeling isolated and resentful. Talking to others can help you to feel accepted and hopeful.

If you have bought into the myth that sex offenders are all hopeless and can't be helped, that will make it all the more difficult for you to admit that your partner is a sex offender. Keep in mind that society has always sensationalized people's problems. Today, newspaper writers point to any relapse by a sex offender as "proof" that sex offender treatment is worthless.

The reality is that, just as with alcohol and drug treatment, there are treatment failures and treatment successes. The key for the offender—and for his partner—is acknowledging the problem and learning to understand it, accept it, and prevent it from happening again.

A second type of denial occurs when offenders or family members deny their awareness of sexual abuse by saying they didn't know what was happening. Some men will admit the facts of what they've done but will say that the crime occurred while they were drunk or high on drugs, and they didn't know what they were doing. Substance abuse does sometimes play a role in sexual crimes, but people do not do things under the influence of drugs that they haven't thought about doing before. Being drunk or stoned may lower their inhibitions to doing certain things or make them careless about the consequences, but it never puts the idea into their head! The idea was already there. The intoxication only lets it out. Many men who commit sex crimes while intoxicated purposely get intoxicated so they can feel freer to go ahead and do what they want to do.

Some men say they didn't know that what they did was against the law. Some say they didn't know how old their victim was. But we all choose to ignore things we don't want to think about, don't we? If a man didn't know how old his victim was, it was because he didn't want to know. He didn't ask. The truth is that we all know that having sexual contact with a child, rape, and exposing are against the law. Your partner may have told himself that others have committed the same crime and gotten away with it. He probably believed he would get away with it too.

Denial of awareness by nonoffending parents sometimes goes on for a long time before the abuse becomes known. For some women, it is a way for them to survive. Now, maybe for the first time, you can be completely honest with yourself. Think back: Were there clues you might have noticed while the sexual abuse was happening, clues you couldn't stand to think about because what they suggested was too horrifying? Most women, in looking back, recognize that they were denying some things to themselves. You don't have to blame yourself if you denied: Denial is what people do when confronted with things too painful to accept.

> "One night, he wanted to take my 13-year-old daughter to see a movie. I said, what about me? I felt left out and angry. I was even jealous. Then, a few weeks later, my daughter begged to sleep over at her cousin's house. I thought she just wanted to play . . . now, I know she was trying to get away from her father."

Even some victims will deny that they were aware of the abuse. They might say they were asleep and didn't know it was happening. This is their way of trying to protect themselves from the shame of having been abused. They are afraid that others will think they "caused" it to happen, "allowed" it to happen, or participated in the abuse. They often believe—wrongly—that they did something to invite the abuse.

Another type of denial is denying the impact of sexual abuse on the victim. This occurs when people minimize the effect that sexual abuse has on the child. Maybe you believe the victim wasn't really hurt by what happened or that it wasn't as bad as everyone is making it out to be. Many men begin treatment holding onto beliefs that if they didn't penetrate a victim, they didn't really hurt him or her. Mothers might see a child who is doing well in school and seems to be happy and say, "she's over it." The truth is that sexual assault is harmful to victims in many different ways. You will learn more about those different harmful effects when you get to the chapter on how sexual abuse affects children. Right now, it is important to accept that your child is hurting. Sexual assault is about power and control, and the sexual abuse violated your child and stole something from her.

> Renee's husband was charged with touching the breasts of her 13-year-old daughter, Tanika. One day soon after the disclosure, they were watching Oprah together, and the show was about a woman who had been brutally raped by her father for years. Renee turned to Tanika and said, "at least that didn't happen to you . . . you were lucky." Tanika didn't feel very lucky. She felt that her mother didn't understand how hurt, betrayed, and scared she was. She felt that her mother thought being fondled was no big deal. So the next time she was interviewed by her social worker, she told the social worker that her father had raped her. He went to prison for 3 years. Years later, Tanika admitted that she had embellished the allegations only so that her mother would pay attention to her pain.

Denying that the perpetrator was responsible for causing the abuse is still another type of denial. Responsibility for sexual abuse always lies solely with the perpetrator, who is an adult and knows right from wrong. When people mistakenly assign responsibility for the abuse to someone or something else, they are denying the responsibility of the offender.

The offender might be saying that it wasn't his fault because his wife or girlfriend drove him to it by not having sex with him. Or he may accuse the victim of "coming on to him" or being "willing." Younger children are usually willing to go along with anything adults suggest because they are taught to respect and obey adults. Sometimes, teenagers are in a hurry to be grown up, and they want to experiment with sex. But neither younger children nor teenagers are capable of making decisions about sex because they can't fully understand the consequences of those decisions. A parent's job is to provide guidance to teenagers who are in too much of a hurry and are getting in over their heads—not to exploit them. By blaming his victim, an offender is continuing the exploitation.

Sometimes, offenders blame their sexual abuse on substance use. They say it was the drugs that made them do it, that if they weren't drinking or drugging, they wouldn't have offended. As we discussed, drinking and drugging are usually just tools offenders use to make it easier for them to let out their deviant desires and then use as an excuse for their behavior. Millions of people use alcohol and other substances without victimizing children.

You might also have blamed yourself, the victim, the system, or substances for your partner's behavior or his arrest. Sometimes, victims blame themselves for not saying "no" and stopping the abuse. Sometimes, they then blame themselves again for telling and getting the abuser in trouble. When victims blame themselves, it only adds to the injury they have already suffered. They need someone who understands what they have been through to assure them that it wasn't their fault. If you have blamed *anyone or anything* besides the abuser, you have been denying the offender's responsibility.

Probably the most common type of denial among sex offenders is denying the need for treatment. Many men come to treatment claiming they have no need for therapy. They insist that they have learned their lesson, that they won't use substances any more and therefore won't reoffend, that they would never risk going to prison again, that they now know something that they didn't know before, or that they don't have access to children anymore. But the truth is that none of these factors by themselves will prevent anyone from reoffending. In fact, there is no way—even with treatment—that an offender can ever guarantee he won't do it again. The only way for him to have a good chance at not reoffending is to fully acknowledge that he has an attraction to children, to become aware of what led to his loss of control, and to learn how to change his distorted style of thinking and acting. These are major changes that don't happen overnight and don't happen just because a man decides he doesn't like jail.

Nonoffending parents often feel that they don't need treatment because they didn't do anything wrong. But treatment isn't punishment for the offender or the partner. Treatment offers support, education, insight, and healing. Treatment is about getting your life back under control. Anyone who has been through any experience as traumatic as the one you've been through can usually benefit from therapy.

Denial can be very strong—and very convincing. Remember, denial is a way that we protect ourselves from acknowledging threatening truths. Some women have held onto their denial even after the offender admits to committing the sexual abuse!

Reasons why a nonoffending parent may deny that sexual abuse occurred:

> She feels that she has to choose between the child and the perpetrator.
> She loves both and feels torn between them.
> She feels ashamed to admit she couldn't protect her child.
> She loses trust in herself and her own judgment.
> She may feel that the abuse is a reflection on her own sexuality or attractiveness.

As June and Richard sat in the therapist's office, he admitted to her for the first time that he had, in fact, molested their four-year-old daughter. "No," she said, shaking her head. "I know you are just saying that to comply with the therapy program. I know you didn't really do it." Richard and the therapist looked on in disbelief as June continued to insist that she knew it was all a big misunderstanding.

She may wonder, why did he choose a child over me?
She may fear losing financial security (even in an upper-middle-class home).
She may fear child protection agency involvement.
She may fear being blamed.
She feels emotionally dependent on the abuser.
She may be afraid of the perpetrator.
She may be ashamed of her choice of mate.
She was sexually abused herself, and the current situation brings up painful memories.
She was not protected from abuse in her own family growing up and doesn't know how to protect her child.
She makes her own attempts to protect the child.
She believes she can handle it on her own.

Reasons why the offender may deny that abuse took place:

He feels ashamed, he knows its wrong.
He wants to stop but doesn't know how.
He thinks he can handle it himself.
He doesn't want to give up the pleasure he gets from sexual abuse.
He can't admit he's out of control.
He wants to avoid jail or prison.
He wants to avoid a child protection investigation.
He is afraid he will lose his family if they know what he really did.
He cant admit that he is a sex offender.

Reasons why a child might deny that abuse took place:

She thinks she did something wrong and will get in trouble.
She doesn't want to get the abuser in trouble. (She may love him!)
She is afraid that her family will be mad because she told.
She is afraid of being sent away to a foster home.
She has sometimes been threatened by the abuser.
She believes her parents are mad at her for causing the abuse.
She is afraid of losing her mother's love.
She feels she "participated" in the abuse by not telling sooner.
She feels ashamed and conflicted because her body responded to the sexual stimulation.

TABLE 2.1 Examples of Denial

Type of Denial	Offender	Nonoffending Parent	Child
Denial of the facts	I didn't do it.	It couldn't happen in my family. It's all a misunderstanding.	I made it up, it didn't really happen. He was only bathing me.
Denial of awareness	I was drunk and didn't know what I was doing. I didn't know how old she was.	I worked at night and never saw anything unusual. The child never told me anything.	I was asleep.
Denial of responsibility	The child was wearing sexy clothes. The child wanted to learn about sex.	I told her not to walk around without a bra. She came on to him.	I should have said no. I should have made him stop.
Denial of impact	I didn't really hurt her. I never forced her. She liked it.	She'll get over it, she seems to be doing OK.	It didn't really bother me that much.
Denial of the need for treatment	I learned my lesson by going to prison.	Now that I know, I'll watch him more carefully.	I don't want to talk about it.

SOURCE: Modified from Trepper, T. S., & Barrett, M. J. (1989). *Systemic Treatment of Incest, a Therapeutic Handbook.* New York: Brunner/Mazel.

A disclosure of sexual abuse creates many feelings for family members: fear, anger, betrayal, and a desire to protect each other from consequences. The disclosure leads to a crisis, and during a crisis, everyone's goal is to get back to normal. They may believe that if they ignore it, it will go away. They may want only for things to go back to the way they were before the disclosure.

In Table 2.1, you will find examples of how each family member might display the different types of denial. These examples might include a statement that the family member might make, or it may describe their thoughts.

WORK SHEET #2: DENIAL

Fill in the chart by giving examples of how your family displayed the different types of denial. You may quote a statement that the family member might have made or describe what their actions suggested to you.

Type of Denial	Offender	Nonoffending Parent	Child
Denial of the facts			
Denial of awareness			
Denial of responsibility			
Denial of impact			
Denial of the need for treatment			

CHAPTER 3

How Sexual Abuse Affects Children and Families

Child sexual abuse is any sexual touching, fondling, oral-genital contact, or rape of a child by an adult. For an adult to expose his or her genitals in a sexual way or to "peep" at an undressed child in a sexual way is abuse. *Any kind* of sexual activity between an adult and a child under 18 is child abuse. Using a child for one's own sexual pleasure is sexual abuse.

Sexual assault victims often experience long-lasting emotional pain from their abuse. They feel hurt, angry, and helpless. Frequently, they blame themselves because they feel they should have done something to stop or prevent the assault. Some victims feel different from other people all their lives and never learn to have healthy, fulfilling relationships. Most victims struggle with liking and accepting themselves. Nothing crushes a child's self-esteem like being abused.

Sexual assault hurts not only the victim but the victim's family and friends. All the victim's relationships can be damaged because the victim has trouble trusting again. The victim may become withdrawn and distant. Loved ones may feel helpless to take away the victim's pain. Future relationships are affected because the sexual assault changes the way the victim sees the world and relates to others.

Children who have been sexually assaulted may experience
     Behavior problems
     Aggression
     Withdrawal
     Nightmares
     School problems
     Self-blame
     Isolation, feeling different
     Confusion

Children who are being sexually abused must try to adapt to their situation. They must survive in what to them is a bizarre new world. In many ways, they feel trapped and paralyzed. Frequently, they do not tell anyone what is happening. They may deny the abuse when asked about it because they want to protect the perpetrator, who is often someone they know and love. They may deny the abuse because they feel they have done something wrong by "participating" in it and they will be blamed for it. They may not want to lose the love, attention, and affection the offender provides during the course of the abuse.

Children adapt in different ways. Some children become shy and withdrawn so as not to draw attention to themselves. They have learned that attention leads to abuse. Other children become seemingly seductive and appear to seek out the abuse. For these children, the abuse may be tolerable if it represents the only attention or affection they receive.

Some children look for approval from other adults and try to be "extra" good to make up for their bad feelings from the abuse. More commonly, however, victims misbehave, trying to force the adults around them to notice that something is wrong. Many teenage victims turn to smoking, stealing, drugs and alcohol, skipping school, hanging out in gangs. As their lives feel increasingly out of control, they may seek to numb their feelings, to escape from their painful environment at home, and to strike back at their parents by getting into trouble. They may also become sexually promiscuous, as they have learned that sex provides them with attention from others and at least a few minutes of pleasure. Any and all of these self-destructive "acting-out" behaviors should be indicators to a parent that something serious is wrong in the life of their child. Unfortunately, it's sometimes easier and safer for parents to just assume they have a "bad kid" or to blame their child's problems on associating with the wrong crowd.

Children are easily abused because

     They are eager to please.
     They trust adults.

They are taught to obey adults.

They are dependent on adults for physical and emotional needs.

Most children blame themselves for the abuse. Because children are told in school that sexual touching by an adult is bad, many children believe that they have done something bad by "letting" an adult touch them. Some feel guilty because the sexual activity felt physically pleasurable. Victims often feel that their bodies betrayed them. Their body, of course, was reacting to touch just like it is supposed to. It is the abusive adult who betrayed the child.

Adults know right from wrong. Children depend on adults to do the right thing. When adults do things that children know are wrong, the children begin to lose trust in the adults that they depend on for their survival. When abusers deny that abuse occurred, child victims begin to think they are crazy because their reality is being challenged. When other adults fail to protect them, children begin to believe that they can't count on others. They learn that no one will really take care of them. Nothing could be more frightening for a child.

> When Susan told her mother that her stepfather had been touching her in her bed at night, her mother immediately confronted him. Susan stood by in helplessness and despair as she watched her stepfather heatedly deny the abuse and blame her for trying to "run him out of the house." Her mother then punished her for lying, and Susan knew that the abuse would continue.

What Are the Effects of Child Sexual Abuse?

Child sexual abuse can lead to drug and alcohol abuse, eating disorders, self-destructive behavior, teenage pregnancy, depression, and suicide. Children who are sexually abused may experience strong feelings of powerlessness, shame, mistrust, and alienation (feeling different from others). Adult survivors report feeling a lot of shame and mistrust.

If one was molested as a child, he or she may have never developed a healthy sense of "boundaries." Victims may not learn how to say "no" to people, and they may find themselves being abused again as adults. Or they may keep a distance from everybody to protect themselves and never have any meaningful relationships.

For some victims, events that happen following the physical act of sexual abuse can be almost as damaging as the abuse itself. These children may be doubly traumatized by

Telling and not being believed or protected
Being removed from their homes
Being told by other adults to keep secrets
Being accused of betraying the family
Being returned to a home without protection, allowing the abuse to continue
Having to testify against someone they love

The more often the sexual abuse occurred, the more damaging and long lasting the effects will usually be. Similarly, abuse that took place over long periods of time is typically more traumatic than abuse that ended quickly. The severity of the abuse means the extent of the sexual contact. The more severe the abuse, the more devastating it will usually be. This does not mean that fondling is necessarily less severe than penetration but that the type of sexual ac-

Factors That Affect the Impact of Sexual Abuse on a Child

Frequency of the abuse (how often it happened)

Duration of the abuse (how long it went on)

Severity of the abuse (the type of physical sexual contact)

Violence, force, threats, or physical pain during the abuse

Age of the child

The closeness of relationship with the abuser

Events that follow the disclosure (such as any of those listed above)

tivity is one important factor that will contribute to the child's reaction.

The closer a child is to the abuser, the more traumatic the abuse will usually be. In other words, the more dependent the child is on the abuser, the greater is the betrayal and the child's resultant helplessness. Children abused by family members are usually greatly affected by the abuse. When children are abused by strangers, they tend to get greater support from family, friends, and authorities. This is because the family does not have a relationship with the abuser and feels no loyalty conflict. The support a child receives helps him or her through the trauma.

Young children are sometimes unaware that they are being abused. Abusers may touch preschool children in a sexual way that seems to be part of normal interactions, such as bathing, dressing, or diapering. The youngster may not show any immediate symptoms, but might suffer from the abuse in later years, when he or she realizes what was happening.

When violence, force, physical pain, or lethal threats are involved in sexual abuse, the degree of trauma a child experiences is usually enormous. When children fear for their lives or the lives of others they love, they may be overwhelmed and unable to cope with this brutality.

Sheila was 6 years old when her stepfather began coming into her room at night to sexually abuse her. He also physically abused her, frequently hitting her with his fists. One day, he took her into the yard, where the cat had just had kittens. Picking up one of the tiny kittens, he squeezed its neck while it kicked its little feet until it died. He looked straight into her eyes and said quietly, "that's what will happen to you if you tell." A year later, 7-year-old Sheila tried to kill herself by jumping out of a window. She was in a psychiatric hospital from age 12 to 17.

Victims of sexual assault find that their world has become an unpredictable and frightening place. They begin to believe that nothing is what it seems and that they have lost any control over their life. Later, closeness, intimacy, and sexual contact may bring flashbacks of the abuse. Victims who knew and loved their abuser may feel guilty and ashamed about sex all their lives.

A doctor named Roland Summit discovered that many sexually abused children display a common pattern of behavior and feelings in response to sexual abuse. He called this pattern the "child sexual abuse accommodation syndrome."[1] Dr. Summit described the following predictable sequence of events that trap the victim and compound his or her suffering:

Stage 1: Secrecy. The offender befriends the child, gains her trust, abuses her, and convinces her not to tell. The child is scared and confused both by the sexual acts and by the fact that the acts have to be kept secret. Sometimes the offender threatens the victim with physical harm if she tells. Most often, the threats are not violent but vague, suggesting to the child that "something bad" will happen if anyone else learns about the sexual abuse.

Stage 2: Helplessness. The child feels powerless to stop the abuse. She feels she cannot turn to anyone for help. The child gives in to the abuse to please the abuser and to ward off the "something bad" that has been threatened if she tells.

Stage 3: Accommodation. The child tries to accept the abuse by believing the abuser's excuses and lies. The child turns off her feelings. The child adjusts to the abuse in any way she can. For instance, a child may become "seductive" and behave in a way that she hopes will bring love or affection.

Stage 4: Disclosure. The child tries to tell, often in a vague, confused, and unconvincing way. She might be testing the waters to see what will happen if she tells. If the response is protective, the child may continue to disclose. If nobody believes her, or if the person she has told calls her liar, or if the adults seem upset by her disclosure, she may simply stop talking about the abuse.

Stage 5: Recantation. "Recanting" means taking it all back or changing the story. Not all children recant, but many do. The child may feel pressure to deny the abuse based on the crisis it has created for her family. The victim is willing to sacrifice herself to protect the family. *Recantation is a normal and expected part of the painful disclosure process.* It should *not* be interpreted to mean that the abuse never happened. Many families latch onto the recantation in the desperate hope that they can, after all, make the whole thing go away. In buying into the recantation, the family then sees the victim as a lying, bad child who maliciously created the crisis. If the victim has been acting out in other ways, it is easy to believe this picture of a bad child and use it to reinforce denial of the crime. In doing so, the family risks revictimizing the child in a terribly hurtful way.

You and your family may have lost a great deal because of the sexual abuse, including money and time spent fighting your partner's legal battles. The children may have become stigmatized by your partner's behavior. Your family probably feels ashamed, embarrassed, and isolated. They may be humiliated in their community.

If the perpetrator denied his crimes, the victim no doubt felt that she was being punished. She might have been blamed, doubted, subjected to intrusive medical exams, removed from her home, or even encouraged to change her story to protect the abuser. This denial was another abuse to the victim.

Your child needs you to understand what the sexual abuse meant to her and to recognize that the impact of the abuse is only partly related to the physical sexual activity that took place. Your child needs you to relate to the feelings she has about the abuse and to realize that it has changed her life forever.

What Your Victimized Child Probably Needs From You

Do	*Don't*
Tell your child it wasn't his or her fault	Restrict your child's activities more than necessary
Ask what your child needs to feel safe; for example, a night light	Make too many changes right after the disclosure
Let your child know it's OK to be confused	Minimize your child's feelings
Let your child know you aren't mad	Ask probing questions about the abuse; let the child talk freely
Realize it's OK to let your child know you're sad or to see you cry	Make promises you can't keep
Keep your child informed about what might happen	Urge the child to forget it
	Question your child's story
Let your child know the abuser was at fault	Evade your child's questions
Reassure your child that you want to protect him or her	Let your child blame him or herself
	Tell your child not to talk about it
Ask your child about his or her feelings	

There may be times when the victim seems OK and shows no symptoms. At other times, your child might seem worried, scared, or angry. These mood swings are normal. Reassure your child; be firm but gentle, and let your child talk about the abuse as little or as much as she wants. Take your child to see a therapist who specializes in sexual abuse so that recovery and healing can begin right away.

Depending on the age of your child, the effects of the sexual abuse will vary. Sometimes, small children seem to resolve the trauma easily but need additional therapy in their teen years as they become more sexually aware. In the later teens and early adulthood, many abused children have difficulties with relationships and intimacy. Support your child over the years in any way she needs.

Some children and teens exhibit very obvious signs of trauma, such as anger, self-destructive behavior, substance use, and rebelliousness. Sexual abuse creates enormous confusion for kids (especially those who don't receive the proper therapy), and these feelings may be played out through their behavior. Other children seem fine and may even become overachievers. This apparent normalcy can be misleading—don't assume that your child isn't hurting.

> "As a teenager, I was a cheerleader and got near straight As. I was popular and involved in every activity possible. My parents assumed I hadn't been affected by the abuse. What they didn't know was that I *had* to keep busy so that I didn't have time to feel anything. I stayed active to get away from all my bad feelings. Whenever I stopped moving, I started hurting again."

> "As a child, I had always taken gymnastics lessons. In high school, I was on a team and competed nationally. I was driven to win. Everyone commented on how mature and dedicated I was. The truth was that while I was being abused, I had always felt like I was bad and was doing something wrong. The gymnastics became a way to be good. I was trying to make up for being such a bad little girl."

What Your Child Needs to Hear From You to Reduce Shame and Guilt . . .

He tricked you.
He knew better.
It wasn't your fault.
I know you didn't want to get anyone in trouble.
I'm glad you told.

Our family troubles aren't your fault.

I'm sorry I didn't protect you.

I'm proud of your wonderful qualities.

I'll try to keep you safe.

Boy Victims Often Have Special Needs

As you may have noticed, in this book we have referred primarily to girls as the victims of sexual abuse. Our focus on girl victims does not mean that boys are not also sexually abused—they certainly are. However, boy-oriented child molesters rarely make good candidates for family reunification, because they are generally more dangerous than girl molesters. They have more victims and they are likely to reoffend. If your son has been molested, he needs your care, love, and understanding every bit as much as a daughter would. In fact, he may be struggling with additional issues that you should be aware of.

Boys who are victimized by older male abusers may experience other disturbing feelings in addition to the ones already discussed. Boys who are entering puberty may be especially vulnerable to the advances of sexual predators because they are already experiencing hormonal changes that make them eager to "experiment" with new sexual activities. Later, after they have participated in the abuse, they may find themselves crushed under the weight of conflicts and confusion they did not anticipate and cannot resolve.

Boys abused by men may end up questioning their sexual orientation for the rest of their lives. Because the abuse often is their first sexual experience, if their bodies responded to the physical pleasures of sexual touching, they are left wondering if they are homosexual. This doubt can create a host of other disturbing feelings, including shame, isolation, and stigmatization. Boys are often afraid to tell of sexual abuse by males for this very reason—they fear being labeled as homosexuals.

Sex offenders who molest boys know these things, of course. They use the child's growing interest in sexuality as a way to introduce abusive sexual activity. They also take advantage of their victims' reluctance to tell anyone about the abuse. If your son has been molested by a male abuser, try not to respond with shock or disgust. Reassure him that he is normal and, with the help of a therapist who specializes in child sexual assault, help him understand how his normal feelings were used against him.

Some books about the sexual abuse of boys that might be helpful for you to read include *Victims No Longer*, by Mike Lew; *From Victim to Offender*, by Freda Briggs; and *Abused Boys*, by Mic Hunter.

If your daughter was victimized as a child and is now an adult, the book, *Allies in Healing*, by Laura Bass and Ellen Davis, provides suggestions for how you can support her in her recovery.

As you do the following exercises, you might find that it is hard to know how your child or your partner's victim was feeling. If you were sexually abused yourself, you can draw on your own experience to help you understand how the victim feels. If you were not sexually abused, think about some other experience in which you were victimized or felt powerless, such as being physically abused, being the victim of a violent crime, or another experience that was out of your control. These are difficult exercises. Take some time to think about them.

EXERCISE 3.1

Read the following vignette, and think about the feelings this child experienced during and following sexual abuse.

Twelve-year-old Darby was fondled on her breasts and kissed by her oldest brother, age 20, several times over a 3-month period. Feeling unsure of what to do, she wrote a letter to her godmother explaining the situation. Her godmother discussed it with a friend who worked in a school and he, as a mandated reporter, reported the incidents to the local social service agency.

Social workers and police investigated. Darby's mother was at first shocked and reluctant to believe what was being alleged but when she confronted her son, he admitted to the accusations and promised not to do it again. Darby felt relieved and thought that now that her mother was aware of her brother's behavior, the abuse would not recur. She didn't want her brother to go to jail; she just wanted the abuse to stop.

When the police returned to question Darby, she told them that the whole thing had been a mistake and that nothing had happened. The police officer made her write a letter of apology to her family and threatened to arrest her for filing a false report.

EXERCISE 3.2

Read the following vignette and think about the feelings this child had during her abusive childhood. Think also about the ways in which her abuse probably affected her life.

Jenny was 3 years old the first time her stepfather sexually molested her. The abuse continued for years, worsening in frequency and severity, and by the time Jenny was 7, her stepfather was having frequent vaginal intercourse with her and forcing her to perform oral sex on him. He was also physically abusive, beating her often, as was Jenny's mother.

One day, Jenny put a pair of underpants that were wet with her stepfather's semen in the hamper. Jenny's mom found them and questioned Jenny. When Jenny tried to explain to her mom what her stepdad had been doing to her, her mother scolded her for urinating in her pants and then lying about it.

At age 9, Jenny revealed to her health teacher in a sex education class that her stepfather was abusing her. Investigators questioned Jenny's stepfather before getting a statement from her. He convinced them that Jenny was a rebellious child with a wild imagination and was just trying to get attention. After the investigators left, Jenny's stepfather turned on the stove and sat Jenny on top of it, burning and scarring her buttocks. He warned her that she had better not try reporting him again.

EXERCISE 3.3

Read the following vignette and think about the ways in which this victim was harmed.

Fourteen-year-old Lauren was molested by her father from age 7. Although there was medical evidence of anal injuries, her father denied the allegations and was never arrested. Instead, Lauren was placed in foster care, forcing her to change schools and lose her friends. She felt completely alienated from her family.

Lauren actually had a closer relationship with her father than her mother. She lost this relationship when she was placed in foster care. Her mother does not believe that the abuse ever occurred and believes that Lauren fabricated the allegations after arguing with her father about not being allowed to date boys. Her mother frequently states that Lauren has destroyed the family and subjected them to financial ruin. Lauren's two brothers have been told that she was removed from the home because she is a liar.

Lauren, alone and depressed, wishes she had never said anything to anyone. Although she hated being sexually abused, she loves her father and now feels she has lost her entire family.

EXERCISE 3.4

Read the following vignette and think about the reasons why child abuse is never the victim's fault.

Jeff was 4 years old when his uncle began to wrestle with him and fondle him in a sexual way. At first, Jeff didn't even notice. When his uncle began asking him to undress and perform sexual acts with him at age 5, Jeff felt something was wrong. But his uncle convinced him that their "little secret" was a special bond between them and that if anyone else knew, they wouldn't understand and bad things would happen. Jeff liked the attention and treats he got from his uncle and, after all, the sexual touching felt good.

When Jeff was 8 years old, his mother walked in on them and immediately called the police. She barred the uncle from having any further contact and supported Jeff in helping him understand that what happened wasn't his fault. Jeff testified at the trial, and his uncle was convicted and sentenced to 20 years in prison.

As an adult, Jeff is extremely conflicted about his sexual orientation. He is attracted to women but finds himself also thinking about men in sexual ways. Although he knows his parents acted appropriately and protectively, he feels guilty for "sending" his favorite uncle to prison. He has been told that the abuse was not his fault, but he knows, deep down, that the sexual touching felt good and that he went along with it. He continues to live in fear, waiting for something bad to happen, as his uncle promised. As an adult, he knows his fear is irrational, but he can't help feeling anxious all the time.

Note

1. Summit, R. C. (1983). The Child Sexual Abuse Accommodation Syndrome. *Child Abuse and Neglect, 7*, pp. 177-191.

WORK SHEET #3: EFFECTS OF SEXUAL ABUSE ON CHILDREN

Thinking about your own child or your partner's other victim, describe at least eight (8) feelings you think the child experienced during and following the sexual abuse.

_____

_____

_____

_____

_____

_____

_____

_____

_____

_____

_____

Thinking about your child or your partner's other victim, describe at least five (5) feelings the child may have had since the abuse stopped.

_____

_____

_____

_____

_____

_____

_____

_____

_____

_____

_____

Thinking about your child or your partner's victim, describe at least eight (8) ways in which the victim was harmed.

_____

_____

_____

_____

_____

_____

_____

_____

_____

_____

_____

_____

Thinking about your child or your partner's victim, describe at least five (5) reasons why child abuse is never the victim's fault.

_____

_____

_____

_____

_____

_____

_____

_____

_____

_____

_____

_____

_____

CHAPTER
4

Signs and Symptoms of Sexual Abuse in Children

Children show many different signs and symptoms of sexual abuse. In this chapter you will learn the different signs to look for if you think your child might be being abused. *Understand that just because a child displays one or more of these symptoms, it does not necessarily mean they are being sexually abused.* Some of the behaviors are ones that any child might display on occasion. Some of the behaviors might be a reaction to some other traumatic event in the child's life. For instance, many children go through periods of having nightmares; by itself, this symptom should not be taken to mean that sexual abuse has occurred.

Certainly, the most obvious indicator of sexual abuse is when a child makes a statement that he or she is being abused. Children rarely make up stories about sexual abuse. Young children don't know enough about sexual behavior to talk about it if they haven't had direct experience with it. Sexual offenders like to claim that children make false accusations based on information they have received from television or movies. The truth is, of course, that television and general release movies, no matter how sexually suggestive they may be, do not provide explicit sexual information. If a child has been exposed to hard-core pornography, that in itself is sexual abuse.

Do not discount what your child says. Ask questions and clarify information. If your child makes a statement about being abused, contact local authorities or a mental health professional experienced in sexual abuse so that the child can be interviewed properly.

Children can be confused about events that have happened to them. If your child tells you something that sounds unusual or confusing, ask for details and try to clarify what happened (without suggesting *anything*). Let your child explain what he or she means in their own words. Some of the things that children say may sound suspicious at first, but after careful consideration, turn out to be innocent.

> A 3-year-old had diarrhea. He was in a lot of pain going to the bathroom and his bottom was red and irritated. He was crying and wouldn't let his mother put Desitin on his buttocks, so his mother held him down while his father put the cream on. The next day the child told his teacher, "My butt hurts. My mommy held me down and my daddy put his finger in my butt. White stuff came out on me." Although this statement initially sounded very suspicious of sexual abuse, after careful investigation the actual events were clarified.

How Do I Know if My Child Is Really Telling Me About Sexual Abuse?

Did the child make a *spontaneous*, unprompted disclosure?

Does the story stay the same over time? Are the details consistent? Does the logic of the story make sense?

Does the statement have sensory details, including smells, tastes, feelings, times, descriptions of places, and so on?

Does the child exhibit behavior or knowledge beyond what is appropriate for the age of the child? For instance, children can't describe the process of the erection of a penis unless they've experienced it. If they are talking about an adult's erect penis or about licking a penis or about white stuff coming out of a penis, they are clearly describing events beyond what you would expect them to know.

Is there other evidence that supports your child's story? For instance, if a witness saw the abuse, or if the abuser admits touching the child on her genitals while denying sexual intent, or if the abuser has been accused of sexual abuse before, these facts strongly suggest that your child's story is not made up. Medical evidence occasionally can confirm that genital injury has occurred (but most sexual abuse does *not* leave marks or injuries, so the absence of medical evidence does *not* mean that sexual abuse hasn't occurred). Polygraphing (giving a "lie-detector test" to) the alleged abuser has been shown to be an excellent way to clarify conflicting evidence of sexual abuse.

The best thing you can do if you suspect abuse is to report the abuse to your local child welfare agency and let experienced professionals investigate to determine what really happened. Support your child by listening to her and believing what she says unless and until you have good reason not to.

The emotional and behavioral symptoms that follow are what are called indicators of trauma; most of them are not necessarily specific to sexual abuse. In other words, children experiencing a death, divorce, or even a move to a new house may exhibit many of these same symptoms. One or a few of the signs does not necessarily mean that any trauma has occurred nor does a cluster of symptoms prove that sexual abuse has occurred. Some children have nightmares, some children have an irritable personality, some children cry easily. None of these signs by themselves means that sexual abuse has occurred. However, they form a part of the picture and need to be investigated thoroughly when there are other indicators of sexual abuse.

The one behavior that by itself indicates a high likelihood of sexual abuse is sexual behavior on the part of a child. Although some preschool children masturbate, most school-aged children (age 6-11) do not. Excessive masturbation to the point of irritation, or persisting in public masturbation despite being told not to, should be a cause for concern. And although some preschool children may look at and touch each other's genital areas, they normally do so out of curiosity rather than a sexual intent. Any sexual activity between children that involves penetration or oral-anal-genital contact or that seems to be motivated by a desire for sexual pleasure rather than curiosity is always cause for immediate concern. If your child is forcing, tricking, bribing, coercing, or threatening other children into sexual activity, there is great cause for alarm.

In general, the most important indicators are any unexplained changes in a child's behavior or mood that have continued over time despite your attempts to help your child. Of course, emotional or behavioral symptoms in combination with physical signs of sexual abuse give cause for immediate concern. See Table 4.1 for a more complete list of possible signs and symptoms of child sexual abuse.

Managing Children's Behavior Problems Following Sexual Abuse

Anger and Destructive Behavior

Your victimized child might express a lot of anger. The child might throw things, break things, or hit or be aggressive with other children. Your child might destroy her toys or hurt your pet. Anger is common following sexual abuse. Because the child usually cannot express anger toward the perpetrator, she might direct her anger at others instead. You might be confused when your child seems to take out her anger on you. Don't be angry with your child for being mad. Instead, you can

TABLE 4.1 Possible Signs and Symptoms of Child Sexual Abuse

Physical	Behavioral	Emotional
Pain or itching in genital area	Unexplained changes in behavior	Frequent fantasizing
Difficulty walking, sitting	Withdrawal	Frequent crying
Preoccupation with genitals	Inability to concentrate	Extreme sensitivity
Frequent urinary tract infections	Poor peer relationships	Irritability
Vaginal discharge	Sudden drop in school performance	Mood swings
Painful urination	Secretiveness	Guilt
Bruises or bleeding in genital, oral, or anal areas	Sleep disturbances	Depression
Bed-wetting or soiling	Overcompliance	Fear
Abnormal dilation of vaginal or rectal opening	Delinquency, running away	Hyperactivity
Presence of semen	Child taking on role of wife	Numbness
Sexually transmitted disease	Lack of trust	Shame, worry
Pregnancy	Excessive masturbation	Fear of a particular person
Foreign bodies in genitals	Regressive behavior	Suicidal talk
	Fear of baths	Self-injury
	False "maturity"	Eating disorders
	Change in eating habits	Dissociation
	Aggressive acting out	
	Sophisticated or unusual sexual behavior or knowledge	
	Promiscuity	
	Sexually abuses other kids	

Be firm but gentle in setting limits.

Tell the child what you expect and give a nonviolent consequence for bad behavior (time out or the loss of a privilege); follow through with the consequence.

Tell your child, "It's OK to be angry, but it's not OK to break things, hit, and so on."

Ask your child to tell you about the anger.

Use a lot of "positive reinforcement"—*reward* the child each time she handles anger appropriately.

Reward the good behavior and kind characteristics your child displays (rewards don't have to be material items. Positive attention and praise are often the best rewards).

Withdrawal

Your child might be quiet, clingy, afraid, or distracted after the abuse. Don't try to "correct" the child, or pressure the child to snap out of it. It makes any parent uncomfortable to see their child suffering. But don't let your own discomfort interfere with your ability to support your child in this time of need. Just let your child express her feelings. Give a lot of quiet attention, such as hugs and more time with you. Give the child time to grieve. Reassure the child that she is safe now.

Nightmares and Bed-wetting

Nighttime can be a scary time for a child who has been abused. Especially if the child has been abused in her own room or bed, going to sleep might create a lot of anxiety. Reassure your child, and don't get angry if you seem to be getting less sleep!

Bed-wetting is a common problem following sexual abuse. For children who have been previously dry at night, this is a humiliating experience for them. Make sure a doctor rules out a medical condition, because bed-wetting can sometimes be related to infections or injuries resulting from sexual abuse. If no medical reason exists, begin to modify the child's behavior by providing a reward each time the child wakes up dry. Have children help change the sheets, but don't embarrass them. You can also

> Provide a night-light or leave a light on at night
> Have a sibling sleep in the room with the child
> Designate a stuffed animal to stay awake and "protect" the child
> Reassure the child that she will be safe
> Ask your child to talk about her fears

Sexual Acting Out

Some children who have been sexually abused will engage in sexual behavior with other children. Sometimes, this behavior looks like "sex play"; other times it will involve aggressive or even violent behavior toward other (usually younger) children. If your child seems to be unusually interested in sex, masturbates excessively, tries to touch other children in sexual ways, forces sexual contact with other children, performs sexual acts with animals, or seems to be acting in secret and suspicious ways, seek professional help *immediately*. An experienced counselor can help your child to understand and control these kinds of behaviors.

Medical Examinations

About 90% of sexual abuse incidents leave no physical evidence. Medical exams are most informative when there has been an injury. But fondling, touching, and oral sex—the most common forms of child sexual abuse—will not cause physical injury. Studies have shown that even penetration will not always cause an injury that can be identified in a medical exam. Therefore, an exam by a doctor that concludes that there is no evidence of genital injury should not be assumed to mean that sexual abuse has not occurred. In fact, in most cases, such a medical finding is consistent with the child's story: If the child reported being fondled, for instance, a lack of medical evidence would be expected, because fondling would not injure a child.

Sexually Transmitted Diseases in Children

Sexually transmitted diseases (STDs) are what used to be called "venereal diseases." If your child has been diagnosed with any STD, it is almost certain that your child has been sexually abused. Make sure your child gets the proper medical treatment, as STDs can have serious long-term effects. Any suspected perpetrator should also be tested for STDs, as a positive result can provide corroborating evidence for criminal and family court proceedings.

Gonorrhea	Always transmitted through sexual contact
Syphilis	Always transmitted through sexual contact
Chlamydia	Probable transmission through sexual contact
	Can infect baby through birth canal of infected mother
Genital Warts	Probable transmission through sexual contact
	Can infect baby when infected mother is pregnant
	Transmission through nonsexual direct contact has not been proven
HIV in children	Probable sexual contact if no other risk factors exist (e.g., exchange of blood or HIV mother during pregnancy)
Herpes	Possible sexual contact, birth canal transmission
Herpes II	Probable sexual contact

WORK SHEET #4: SIGNS AND SYMPTOMS OF SEXUAL ABUSE

Think back to the time your child was sexually abused, or ask your partner
about his victim, and list and describe any physical symptoms of sexual abuse.

_____

_____

_____

_____

_____

_____

_____

_____

_____

_____

_____

_____

_____

Think back to the time your child was sexually abused, or ask your partner about his victim, and list and describe at least five (5) emotional symptoms of sexual abuse.

_____

_____

_____

_____

_____

_____

_____

_____

_____

_____

_____

_____

Think back to the time your child was sexually abused, or ask your partner about his victim, and list and describe at least five (5) behavioral symptoms of sexual abuse.

_____

_____

_____

_____

_____

_____

_____

_____

_____

_____

_____

_____

Think back to the time your child was sexually abused, or ask your partner about his victim. Is there anything you realize now that should have seemed unusual or suspicious?

_____

_____

_____

_____

_____

_____

_____

_____

_____

_____

_____

_____

CHAPTER 5

If You Were Sexually Abused as a Child

You might find that one of the most painful parts of dealing with the sexual abuse of your child is that it has reminded you of your own abuse when you were a child. If you were sexually abused, you may have feelings about your own abuse that are now surfacing and that you need to discuss. Feel free to talk about these issues in your group or to request individual sessions with your therapist.

If you were sexually abused, your own abuse may also influence the ways you respond to your child's abuse (or your partner's abuse of another child). For example, without even realizing it, women sometimes are tempted to minimize their child's abuse, or even deny it, because of the terrible power of the feelings that have been reawakened in them. You might feel that now, of all times, you simply can't face these feelings. You wish the feelings would just go away, and so you have tried to make the situation that brought them up go away, too.

You might blame yourself for choosing an abusive partner, for not seeing the abuse while it happened, or for not protecting your child. You might ask, "How could I let this happen? I swore I would never let my child go through what I went through." You might be carrying terrible guilt with you as you attempt to sort through the crisis of the recent abuse while carrying on with your life. It probably all feels overwhelming.

But if you were abused as a child and no one protected you, you never really learned how to be a protective parent. Children learn by doing and seeing. If what you learned as a child was that adults can't or don't protect children from harm, then deep down—without being aware of it—you may still believe that. This thinking may have caused you to feel helpless and powerless when it came to protecting your own child from sexual abuse. Like most sexually abused children, you probably blamed yourself, at least in part, for your own abuse. To blame yourself now, for what your partner did, is to bring back onto yourself some of the most damaging effects of being victimized. If you are blaming yourself, talk to your group or your therapist. *Connections* is about working through these awful feelings. *Don't suffer alone.*

You might want to seek out a support group for adult survivors or find a therapist experienced in treating adults who were abused as children. The book, *The Courage to Heal,* by Laura Davis and Ellen Bass, is a helpful resource for understanding your own abuse. Some other helpful books are *Why Me?* by Lynn B. Daugherty; *Outgrowing the Pain,* by Eliana Gil; and *I Never told Anyone,* by Ellen Bass and Louise Thornton.

You might want to think about whether you should share your own sexual abuse with your child. Sometimes, your child may be comforted by learning that he or she is not alone. You will have to decide if you are ready to talk about the abuse with anyone, let alone your child. Be prepared for the child to ask questions, some of which you might not want to answer. It is OK to choose not to talk about the details of the abuse and instead focus on the feelings you had. You and your child can share your similar feelings with each other.

Some Things You Might Want to Say to Your Child:

I'm sorry this happened to you.

I had a similar experience, so I might have some of the same feelings you do.

Even though we had a similar experience, I know we might *not* have the same feelings.

All feelings are acceptable, all feelings are OK, all feelings are important.

When this happened to me, this is how I felt. Tell me how you feel.

We can get through this together.

Here's what I needed to feel safe. . . . Tell me what you need.

You can talk to me as much or as little as you want to.

I don't really want to discuss the sexual details of what happened, but let me tell you how I felt, and about what happened after.

Don't

Insist that you know how your child feels

Give your child advice about how to handle his or her feelings

Tell your child "now isn't a good time" when she wants to talk

Talk about the sexual details of your own abuse with small children

Generalize that "all men are bad" or "no one can be trusted"

Get angry at your child for asking questions

Say hurtful things about your child's abuser

WORK SHEET #5: IF YOU WERE SEXUALLY ABUSED AS A CHILD

If you were sexually abused as a child, briefly discuss the abuse. Who abused you? Where? When? Did you ever tell? How did others react when you told? How do you think the abuse affected your life?

_____

_____

_____

_____

_____

_____

_____

_____

_____

_____

_____

_____

_____

_____

If you were sexually abused as a child, how do you think your experience might have affected your reaction to your child's abuse or to your partner's disclosure?

_____

_____

_____

_____

_____

_____

_____

_____

_____

_____

_____

_____

CHAPTER
6

Learning About Sexual Offenders

Over the years, experts in the field of sexual deviance have made many attempts to classify child molesters. We say "attempts" because the classification process has never been—and still is not—entirely successful. The reason for this failure is clear: Study after study has shown sex offenders to be heterogeneous, meaning, simply, that they are all different. They are different in age, race, class, ethnicity, religion, education, financial status, and geographic origins. They don't show common symptoms of mental problems (other than their sex offending). They are even different in basic personality traits. Amazingly, no personality test has ever been able to find a difference between child molesters and normal men. In fact, probably the only generalizations that can safely be made about child molesters are these: They are usually men, and they are sexually attracted to children.

There is one label that many experts continue to use to separate child molesters into two types, and that label is pedophile (vs. nonpedophile). The word "pedophile" sometimes gets thrown around loosely these days, but contrary to popular belief, not all child molesters are pedophiles. Experts use the word to refer to men who have a *primary* sexual attraction toward children. These men molest children outside of their families, and they typically have many, many victims. They're what we think of as "sexual predators."

Hopefully, your partner is not a true pedophile but what is called an "intrafamilial" or "incest" offender—a man who responds sexually to a particular child in a particular situation. Incest offenders molest children in their own families or children for whom they have some caretaking responsibility (like stepchildren). The incest offender's victim may or may not be related by blood but is usually a child who knows him well and has feelings for him.

Because no one has sex (or tries to have sex) with someone they are not sexually attracted to, incest offenders obviously have an attraction to children (even though your partner swears to you he doesn't). Usually, though, these men have a primary sexual attraction toward adults. They might be married or in long-term relationships, but they might feel inadequate with their partner and uncomfortable with other adults. If they are unable to develop healthy, fulfilling relationships with their adult partners, they may become affectionate with a child and try to use that child as a substitute for the adult partner they don't feel close to.

Incest offenders typically have fewer victims than pedophiles and usually molest one child at a time. This is not *always* true, however; some men who appear to be incest offenders are actually more interested in children than adults and have had many victims. True pedophiles sometimes will marry women to have access to their children. But even if your partner is not a pedophile, it is important for you to know that as a growing number of sex offender treatment programs across North America have begun to use polygraph examinations to find out more about their clients' backgrounds, *many men who had been thought to have only one victim have been found to have had several—or many—child victims.* These other victims include other family members, friends of their children, neighborhood kids, or children they knew when they were younger. By the time they are caught, *most* child molesters have had other victims and have engaged in a pattern of sexually abusive behavior over a period of years. These are frightening thoughts, we know, and they may be hard for you to believe and accept. "Not *my* partner!" you say, "He's not like that." But how do you really know? Sex offenders are so practiced at manipulating others and hiding their behavior that it is *impossible* to know, simply by talking to them, how many children they have molested.

Find out from your *Connections* therapist or your partner's sex offender treatment provider how polygraphy is used in your partner's treatment program. Although polygraphy is not perfect, it is the best tool we have for uncovering the truth about a sex offender's background. Nowadays, polygraph examiners who specialize in testing sex offenders must take extra training to qualify them for this type of work. If your partner's treatment program hasn't referred him to a specially trained examiner, your *Connections* therapist should be able to locate one for you.

You need to have your partner polygraphed to verify the truth of what he says. A polygraph exam can confirm your partner's claim that he does *not* have a long-standing pattern of abuse and that he really has molested only the victim(s) you know about. Or you might find that your partner has been hiding a long history of sexually deviant behavior, which is critical for you to know if you are planning to bring him into your home. The longer he has been molesting children and the more victims he has had, the more dangerous he is.

You may find that your partner's response to the idea of being polygraphed is revealing in itself. Some offenders immediately protest loudly that the test is unreliable, that it's too expensive, that it's not necessary, or that it's "not admitted in court" (actually, polygraphs are admitted in court under certain circumstances). Your partner may act hurt and angry and complain that you must not trust him if you think polygraphing him is necessary. (Of course, the reality is that you never would have known anything about his problem if he hadn't been caught, right?) Conversely, your partner may state that he's eager to be polygraphed and is "looking forward to it." It's just that he doesn't have the money right now, and there's that other expense that's coming up, and . . . well, he'll get to it as soon as he can because he really *wants* to do it, but . . . don't hold your breath. Some offenders actually drive off to the polygraph office but they get lost on the way, or they forget their wallet, or something else happens to keep them from following through.

In the end, it *must* be done. If your partner fails the exam (is found to be "deceptive"), he needs to go back and take it again . . . and again, if necessary, until he is found truthful. Never forget, a sex offender is *the* best liar you will ever meet. Most offenders have been lying so long and doing it so well they convince themselves they can fool the polygraph examiner. If your partner fails the exam, he will swear he was telling the truth. He will complain that the exam is a scam and the examiner a cheat who just wants his money. He will turn on you and attack you for not believing him and siding with all the people who don't believe him and want to "hold him back." He will challenge your love for him and make you feel guilty for needing to know the truth about him. *And it will all be manipulation.* If he hasn't taken the exam or hasn't passed it, there is a reason for it—and that reason is that he has something to hide.

If you take nothing else from this program, take this: Until your partner has been found truthful on a full-disclosure polygraph examination, *you don't know anything about him.*

Why Do They Do It?

This is not an easy question to answer. Each offender has different reasons for offending, and only he can discover what they are. Understanding his true motivation, in fact, is one of his primary tasks in treatment. He should never use the reasons he comes up with as excuses for his behavior, because sex offending, after all, is always a choice. He needs to understand what motivated him in the past to know what he needs to do now to prevent it from happening again.

Sex offenses are not simply about sex. Usually, offenses represent attempts by the offender to meet emotional needs that he feels powerless to fulfill in adult relationships. These needs may include power, control, attention, affection, nurturing, intimacy, revenge, and expression of anger. Sex becomes the vehicle by which the offender selfishly uses a child for his own physical and emotional gratification. In treatment, your partner should identify the needs he was trying to meet.

Once he better understands his emotional needs, your partner will then need to understand what has blocked him from meeting those needs in his adult relationships. Ultimately, he will need to develop new approaches to creating and maintaining healthy, honest relationships with all the people in his life—his family, his friends, his coworkers—and most important, you. If he is going to be emotionally healthy, he must learn to recognize his emotional needs, express his feelings, communicate his wants, and accept that he cannot blame others for his own unhappiness. He must learn that he cannot fulfill his own needs at the expense of others—especially innocent children.

Grooming

Grooming is the way in which the sex offender sets the stage to abuse a child. It is a process by which the offender manipulates the child and the adults responsible for the child to create opportunities to be alone with the child and abuse her. The steps include gaining the trust of the child, then developing a "special" relationship with the child, and last, manipulating the child into sexual activity. Grooming involves making the child feel important and special by giving her special attention, special privileges, and gifts. The offender singles out his future victim for special attention because he has special plans for her—even though, in his distorted way of thinking, he may deny to himself his attraction or his intention to abuse the child.

The true pedophile often starts the grooming process by winning the trust of his intended victim's parent(s). That means that *everything* this man says and does is a manipulation, aimed at his ulterior motive of getting the child alone. The nonpredatory incest offender is different because he has a genuine relationship with his adult partner and later finds himself attracted to the child. The incest offender showers the child with attention because he is genuinely drawn to her. He may feel affectionate or even "romantic" toward her. But his affection quickly becomes physical, and he starts touching her in nonsexual ways, giving her lots of hugs, tickling her, or sitting her in his lap. As his sexual interest grows, he starts "desensitizing" the child to sexual matters by talking about sex or touching her legs or tickling her around her sexual areas.

As he gradually increases the sexual touching, the offender convinces the child that she is participating in the secret behavior by not rejecting it. The victim may be afraid to reject the sexual contact because she is afraid of losing the affection of this man who has made her feel so special. Very soon, it is too late for the child: By making her feel responsible in part for the increasing sexual activity, the offender makes her a partner in a sexual abuse "conspiracy." Now, the child becomes afraid to tell—she didn't stop it, she reasons, so maybe she will be blamed. She feels trapped and alone. She can't turn to anyone for help, and she is afraid to refuse the offender's requests for sexual gratification for fear that he will leave her, too. *Grooming is an emotional setup that occurs before, during, and after sexual abuse takes place.*

Children are easily manipulated by adults because:

They are eager to please adults.
They trust adults.
They are taught to obey adults.
They are dependent on adults for physical and emotional needs.

Perpetrators become skilled at identifying and preying on vulnerable children. Children who are most vulnerable to being set up by offenders are:

Insecure
Neglected
Unhappy
Craving adult attention or approval
Lonely
Previous victims of sexual or physical abuse
Unsupported by family
Learning disabled
Unsupervised
Exposed to multiple nonfamily caretakers
Kids with parents who are using drugs or alcohol
Foster children

The sexual abuse process is one of gradual seduction. First, the incest offender befriends the child and gains the child's trust. He is the person who is never too busy to play or listen, enjoys activities and games that children want to play, doesn't nag or tell the child "be careful," or "don't get dirty," or "not now," or "don't do that." He may allow a teen to do things parents don't allow, such as smoking, drinking, or viewing pornography. He is the "understanding" adult who becomes the child's buddy, confidant, playmate, and admirer.

Next, the offender showers the child with attention and affection, making the child feel special and important and grateful to the offender. The offender might give the child special privileges, gifts, money, or favors.

Then, the offender engages the child in "intimate" talk, including opening up about his feelings. The child may feel privileged to be included in such grown-up matters. The offender may even fool himself about where this intimacy is leading.

Physical touching sometimes begins with play that seems innocent, such as tickling or wrestling. The offender is feeling out the child to see how comfortable she is with being touched. Often, the child, being sexually naive, is completely unaware of where the touching is leading.

Last, the touching progressively becomes more intimate or sexual (for example, hugging to kissing to fondling to mutual sexual touching). By the time the child realizes that something is wrong, she might have strong feelings of affection for the abuser. And because she has encouraged and enjoyed the abuser's attention and affection, she feels she has played a role in her own victimization.

Suzanne Sgroi, a researcher on sexual abuse, described the six "stages of incest."[1] She studied many sexually abusive families and discovered that, over the long term, incest usually follows a predictable pattern:

1. Engagement: The offender befriends the child, gains the child's trust and the parent's trust, spends a lot of time with the child, and creates a special relationship with the child.

2. Sexual Interaction: Close, affectionate, and loving relationships lead to physical expressions of love (kissing, hugging, touching), which gradually become more sexual in nature.

3. Secrecy: The child becomes trapped in the secret behavior. The offender lets the child know not to tell, sometimes with direct threats, sometimes with more subtle statements, and sometimes by not saying anything but by creating a relationship that the child is afraid to lose.

4. Disclosure: The child makes an attempt to tell. Sometimes, the disclosure is direct and detailed, but other times, it is vague and frightened and unclear. The child is testing the response of the person being disclosed to. If the victim is believed and encouraged, he or she will go on to disclose more.

5. Crisis: Disclosures of sexual abuse always create a crisis. They may bring on legal investigations, family conflict, and mixed emotions.

6. Suppression: If the child is not believed or protected, the child feels betrayed, trapped, helpless, and ashamed. The child may recant his or her accusation (take it back).

Because incest offenders work hard to establish a bond with their victims, they frequently have only to suggest that "Mommy wouldn't understand about our special game" to enlist their victims in a conspiracy of silence. When they feel they have to, however, they will resort to threats. Their threats usually are subtle and vague ("You'll be punished" or "I'll be punished") but sometimes involve physical harm or threats to the victim, her pet, or her family. With young children, it is almost never necessary to apply force. Usually, the offender can easily manipulate his victim to keep the secret.

Some Behaviors to be Concerned About in Your Partner

He treats one child differently from the others, giving her special privileges.

He spends excessive time alone with a child.

He isolates one child from others.

He makes excuses to go places with the child.

He treats the child like an adult.

He "accidentally" walks into bedrooms or bathrooms while the child is undressed.

He walks around naked or "accidentally" lets his private parts show.

He makes occasions to have physical contact with the child, such as bathing or back rubs.

He has secrets with the child.

He "accidentally" touches the child's private parts.

He talks about sex with or in front of the children.

He looks at the child's body or makes comments about the child's development.

He discusses his sex life with his children.

He "teaches" the children sex education.

He "accidentally" allows a child access to pornographic pictures or movies.

He wants to know about your teen's sex life.

The offender often misrepresents, both to himself and others, sexual abuse as normal adult-child behavior. Frequently, the victim is confused by the offender's distortions:

Affection	"At bedtime, my daddy kisses my nose, my tummy, and my kootchie because he loves me all over."
Hygiene	Checking genitals or bottom for "cleanliness"
	Bathing children who are old enough to bathe themselves
Games	Tickling, wrestling, or roughhousing with touching in inappropriate places
Medical treatment	Massages, using creams or ointments on the genitals
Sexual education	"My daddy showed me how to make babies so when I grow up, I can be a mommy."
	"I was teaching my daughter how to enjoy sex with her boyfriend."

Some things offenders tell children:

No one will believe you.

Your mom will be mad at you.

They will think it's your fault.

They'll send you away.

They'll put me in jail.

No one would understand our special relationship.

It would upset your mother.

I'll kill your dog if you tell.

I'll do it to your sister.
It's our special secret.
The monsters will get you.

Most children love their abuser and do not want anything bad to happen to him. They just want the abuse to stop.

Incest Offenders in Treatment

Some typical characteristics of incest offenders:

Low self-esteem
Poor coping skills
Feeling inadequate with adults
Plunging into relationships
Difficulty trusting
Not knowing how to express intimacy needs in other areas of their lives
Poor at resolving conflicts
Opportunistic
Often, law-abiding citizens
Rarely using physical force, but may be coercing child in subtle ways
Probably doesn't have an exclusive sexual preference for children
May see child abuse as sexual experimentation
May have trouble developing truly intimate relationships

Research tells us that incestuous offenders can be helped by treatment and may be less likely to reoffend after treatment than predatory pedophiles. This is good news! With the proper therapy, your partner can learn to control his behavior and prevent future sexual abuse.

Keep in mind, however, that there is no cure for sexual deviancy. Treatment is about controlling one's behavior. Millions of people have destructive addictions to drugs, alcohol, gambling, food, and so on. Nothing can change their attraction to these things, but they certainly can learn not to act on the attraction. Sex offender treatment focuses on teaching abusers how to recognize the situations and feelings that trigger them and put them at risk to offend, how to manage those situations and deal with their feelings, and how to control their urges.

Some reasons why incest offenders do well in treatment:

Their primary sexual preference is for adults.
They generally don't have other criminal tendencies.
Once caught, they want to avoid future negative consequences.
They have more ability to understand the victim's pain.

They are conflicted and ashamed of their behavior and usually have a desire to benefit from treatment (compared to pedophiles).

The fewer victims an offender has, the less the behavior has been reinforced.

Offense Cycles and Chains

In treatment, sex offenders learn to recognize their offense patterns. These predictable patterns include cycles or chains of thoughts, feelings, and behaviors that play a role in setting up and maintaining the abuse. To benefit from treatment, offenders must learn not only to be aware of their patterns but how to change the patterns and stop the cycle of abuse.

The strategy the offender develops in treatment for stopping the cycle of abuse is called his *relapse prevention plan.* His plan will describe the specific steps he will use to control the distorted thinking that leads to abusive behavior. He will also identify his *high-risk factors,* which are the situations, feelings, and places that may stimulate an urge to abuse a child. Before he is ready to graduate from treatment, he will know to stay away from high-risk situations and places, express his feelings appropriately, change his behaviors, and challenge his twisted thinking before it leads him back toward sexually abusing a child.

If you are planning to live with your partner, he will have to share his offense chain or cycle with you, as well as his relapse prevention plan, so that you can better understand him. Later, you will develop a safety plan for your family that is designed to help you and your partner manage the high-risk factors in your home.

You Must Understand
Your Partner's Offense Cycle

Have your partner describe his high-risk factors. Make sure he includes feelings, thoughts, situations, and events that tend to trigger urges for him or jeopardize his ability to control his abusive behavior. He should also be able to explain and give examples of how these factors have contributed to his deviant behaviors in the past. He should be able to list for you all of the types of situations he must now avoid.

Your partner should be able to give examples of how the risk factors fit together with his deviant fantasies and distorted thoughts to form a pattern, cycle, or chain, such as the one pictured in Figure 6.1. He should acknowledge how he has planned his offenses and how he has prepared his victim(s) in the past through grooming behaviors. How has he manipulated other adults

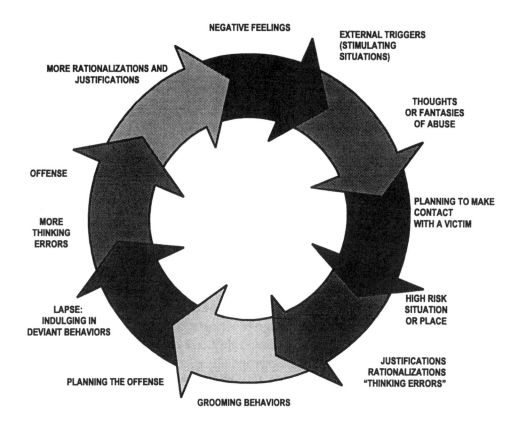

Figure 6.1. Sample Offense Cycle

(including you!) in the past to set up opportunities to offend? How has he made time for offending and created privacy with the victim?

As we discussed earlier, typical grooming behaviors include paying special attention to the victim, giving her special privileges, taking her places, helping with homework, talking about himself, buying presents—all the things that build trust and make the victim feel special. He should describe the ways he tested the waters with his victim through such things as sexual talk, bathing, swimming, tickling, wrestling, and "accidental" touching. He should discuss the past abuse in a way that lets you understand his modus operandi. When he is done, you should have a clear picture of his offense cycle or chain.

Ask the offender to describe some of the distorted thoughts he used to justify and excuse his deviant behavior in the past. He should have no trouble acknowledging how he minimized the harm he was doing, how he placed the blame for his offenses on the victim or on his partner, how he pretended to himself that his victim understood what was happening and wanted it to

TABLE 6.1 Relapse Prevention Factors

Internal	
Thoughts	*Feelings*
What were his distorted thoughts or thinking errors?	What are the feelings that tend to trigger his wanting to offend?
How did he excuse his hurtful behavior in the past?	How does he cope with these feelings now?
How did he convince himself that his victim wanted to be abused or that he was "showing affection"?	If negative feelings arise from a sense of not having his needs met, how does he now attempt to consistently meet his emotional needs through healthy, age-appropriate relationships?
How has he restructured these thoughts into appropriate, healthy thoughts?	

External			
Places	*Situations or Events*	*Stimuli*	*Grooming*
Are there places that he should avoid?	Are there stressful events in his life that trigger urges to offend?	Who or what is he attracted to?	In what ways did he prepare children for sexual assault?
Where should he not go?	How does he avoid these events, if possible?	What sex, age group, or body type?	How did he gain their trust?
Why does he think certain places are safe or unsafe for him in terms of level of risk?	How does he handle them when they arise unexpectedly?	How does he use behavior modification techniques (conditioning exercises he learned in treatment) to control his arousal?	How did he manipulate other adults to have access to kids?
	What other high-risk situations must he avoid?		How did he set up the opportunity to abuse a child?
	How will he avoid them?		What does he do now to stay away from grooming behaviors?
	Under what circumstances does he see himself as able or unable to be around children?		

happen, how he convinced himself that he was really educating the victim or comforting her. Distorted thinking is an important part of the offense chain; the successfully treated offender should have no difficulty admitting how he lied to himself, you, and others and how he used those lies to excuse himself for doing what he wanted to do.

Have the offender talk about the emotional needs he was ignoring or denying in the past that he now knows he must fulfill to stay away from sexually abusing a child. His unmet needs are what have given emotional power to his deviant sexual urges in the past. By learning to recognize and respect his needs now, he can plan on how to fulfill them through healthy relationships—not plan on how to escape from the emptiness that follows their not being met.

Now, looking back to your child's abuse, ask yourself what you might recognize from the offender's description of his abusive patterns? Can you, in retrospect, identify risk factors, such as anger, depression, drinking, or isolating behaviors, that contributed to the offender's secretiveness and withdrawal but that you did not think about at the time? Can you identify grooming behaviors that you ignored, minimized, or denied? Are you now better prepared to know what to look for in your partner that might tip you off that he is in an offending cycle? By the end of this chapter, you should be able to put together many of the pieces of what the offender was thinking, feeling, and doing while he was offending.

What is your partner's relapse prevention plan? Ask him! If he doesn't have a plan, your children aren't safe. His plan should include ways to avoid, escape, and manage high-risk factors. The offender should have several individualized prevention strategies for all of the factors shown in Table 6.1.

Note

1. Sgroi, S. (1982). *Handbook of Clinical Intervention in Child Sexual Abuse.* Lexington, MA: Lexington Books.

WORK SHEET #6: PATTERNS OF OFFENDERS

Looking back at what you now know about your partner or your child's abuser, name and describe at least six (6) characteristics that might have been a sign of his problem.

_____

_____

_____

_____

_____

_____

_____

_____

_____

_____

_____

Looking back at what you now know about your partner or your child's abuser, name and describe at least six (6) behaviors or activities that might have been a sign of his sexual interest in a child or grooming behaviors.

Using the sample offense cycle shown in Figure 6.1 to guide you, fill in your partner's cycle as you understand it.

CHAPTER
7

How to Protect Your Children From Sexual Abuse

Although society would like to believe in the dangers of strangers and take comfort in the idea that children are safe at home, you, tragically, know the harsh truth. The reality is that the vast majority of sexual crimes against children are perpetrated by someone the child knows and trusts, and often these assaults occur right in the child's own home.

Informed, aware parents who make it their business to communicate with their children and with the people who come in contact with their children are best able to protect their children from sexual abuse. All parents should be familiar with the fundamental warning signs of potentially dangerous situations. Beware of men or teenage boys who want to spend a great deal of time with your child, who seem overly generous with your child, or who seek situations in which to be alone with your child (ask yourself why a particular individual is so eager to do you the "favor" of taking your child off your hands).

Men who create many opportunities to be around children (coaching, scout leading, youth group organizing), especially when they have no children of their own, may have suspicious motives. Know where your children are and whom they are with at all times. Carefully check the references of your day care center or babysitter, and do not allow babysitters to bring others into your home. Monitor your child's activity when using the Internet, and discourage your child from using chat rooms, which are used by sexual predators to seek out victims. Caution your child about giving out his or her name, address, or phone number to others on the Internet, and supervise your teen carefully to protect against meetings set up by sexual predators.

In your own home, set a good example of healthy sexuality. Although we focus in this book primarily on physical sexual abuse, inappropriate sexual boundaries can be damaging to children, too. This means that it is important to take care that your child is not exposed to sexual behavior, sexual talk, or sexual material. Make sure that children do not witness adults having sex. Practice modest behavior and respect privacy when dressing and bathing. Do not leave pornographic tapes, magazines, or pictures where children can find them. Even men's magazines, such as *Playboy* or *Penthouse*, can be stimulating and confusing for children. Block adult channels from cable TV, and purchase special software to prevent children from entering sexual sites on the Internet.

Don't talk about your sexual experiences with your children or allow them to overhear such discussions with others. Don't use language that is sexually demeaning or sexually provocative. When children grow up in a home where they are exposed to sexual matters, they become confused. If sex or sexual talk is commonly seen or heard at home, your children will be less likely to interpret sexually inappropriate or abusive behaviors as something they should be concerned about.

Talk to your children not just about stranger danger but about private touching and the right to say "no" to adults. Explain simply that the private parts are the parts of the body that a bathing suit covers and that these parts are special. Let your kids know that if someone wants to look at or touch those parts or asks your child to look at or touch their private parts, that they should assertively say "no." Encourage your child to ask you about any touching or games that seem confusing or unusual.

> A six-year-old girl came home from her first day at summer camp with her wet bathing suit still on. When her mother asked why she didn't change, the youngster replied, "I thought I wasn't supposed to show the other girls my private parts." The mother patiently explained that changing at camp was an exception to the privacy rule.

Teaching children about private touching is tricky. It sometimes seems that for every rule, there is an exception. "Don't let anyone look at or touch your private parts, except . . . the doctor may have to touch you at times, or someone may have to bathe you at times, oh, and also . . . " These exceptions may be confusing, especially to young children. Older children are used to rules that have exceptions. Be aware, though, that offenders are pretty good at convincing kids that what they want to do is an exception to the rule. Children trust adults and expect them to know right from wrong. Sexual perpetrators exploit this trust to manipulate children.

What Children Need to Know to Protect Themselves

Teach your children the signs to look for in someone who might want to abuse them. For example, they should know to be wary of an adult or teenager who seems unusually interested in spending time with them or invites them to engage in activities that purposely exclude others. Traditional commonsense safety measures, such as not talking to strangers or not accepting rides from strangers, are still important. Go a step further, though. Let your child know that dangerous people can look and act just like anyone, that they might invite your child to come and play with their kitten or ask for help finding their lost puppy. With older children, an abuser might try to entice with video games or something forbidden, such as cigarettes or alcohol. Let your child know that the fact that an adult knows their name does *not* mean that adult is not a stranger.

You should teach your children not to go anywhere, even with adults they know, without your permission. Most important, remind your child to say "no" to anything that seems unusual, wrong, sexual, or private and to tell you immediately when these things occur. Remind children that even adults that they know and trust can make mistakes and to tell you about any inappropriate behavior by anyone they know, even family members.

Practice with your child what they could do if anyone approaches them or touches them in any way they don't like. Pretend to be a smooth-talking, manipulative teenager, for example, and apply peer pressure ("Don't be such a baby . . . this is what all the big kids do!"). These lessons will help your child learn to be prepared to be assertive anytime anyone approaches them or touches them in any way that is uncomfortable.

In general, if you ask your children about their activities when they are with others, not in a suspicious or worried fashion but in a curious one, you will be showing your children exactly the kind of attention they need. Children need to know that you are interested in their lives and care about the things that are important to them. Attention makes the child feel close to you, which will improve the chances that your child will confide in you if he or she is worried about something. At the same time, you will be informing yourself about any situations that might require further exploration.

Help your child name five trusted adults (grandparents, teachers, neighbors) that your child could go to for help, if needed. Practice how your child would contact those adults by memorizing phone numbers and by encouraging communication and sharing. Help your child maintain relationships with other trusted adults in their lives. Sometimes, sexual perpetrators say things like, "if you tell your mommy she'll be mad at you." So if the abuser has manipulated your child into being afraid to tell you about the abuse, it is important for him or her to be aware of other adults that can help.

Show your children by example that you are there to help them solve their problems. If they have a problem at school, help them come up with some alternative solutions. If they have problems with friends, talk about some ways to communicate effectively. When your child talks about how he or she feels, don't minimize the feelings ("Oh, it's not so bad"), make fun of them ("Boo-hoo, just like a little baby"), or dismiss them ("There's nothing to be afraid of"). Let your children know that you understand what they feel and that expressing feelings is OK. If necessary, get involved on your child's behalf by talking to a teacher or other individual to help with resolving problem situations.

Above all, listen to your children. Believe what they tell you. Remember, your job is not to frighten your children but to let them know what is unacceptable behavior by others and to be sure that you know what is happening in their lives. Your children need to know that you will be there when they need you, that you will listen to them and trust them, and that you will help them instead of punishing them.

WORK SHEET #7: PROTECTING YOUR CHILDREN

Name and describe at least six (6) things that you can do in the future to prevent sexual abuse of your children. Think in general terms rather than protection from a specific person, because you will be covering that in the next chapter on family safety planning.

_____

_____

_____

_____

_____

_____

_____

_____

_____

_____

CHAPTER
8

Developing a Safety Plan for Your Family

A safety plan is simply a plan of action to keep people safe. For example, many office buildings and schools (and some families) have fire safety plans. Such plans will include strategies to *prevent* fires in the first place, such as rules prohibiting smoking indoors or putting newspapers near a fireplace. They will also include steps to *escape* from a real fire emergency, such as having fire drills and taking planned routes out of a burning building.

Safety plans are often made up of two parts: *prevention* strategies and *intervention* strategies. The prevention part involves the precautions that people will take to try to prevent or avoid an emergency. The intervention part includes the things to be done to escape if a crisis still occurs.

If your children are going to be living with a sexual abuser, you need a safety plan. You need a plan both to minimize the possibility of sexual abuse occurring and to stop it immediately if it should occur.

If you simply assume your child is safe and think you don't need a safety plan, you are engaging in the highest risk behavior there is: denial. Unless you accept, going in, that the potential for sexual abuse exists, you will do nothing to take precautions to prevent it. If you do nothing to prevent it, it is more likely to occur. Although it may still be hard for you to accept the possibility that your partner might abuse your children in the future, not accepting this possibility means risking your children's safety. You will be protecting both your children and your partner by developing a safety plan.

When Is It Safe to Live
With a Known Sex Offender?

This is not an easy question to answer. In fact, the only one who really knows the answer to this question is the sexual abuser himself. Unfortunately, sex offenders often try to convince themselves and others that they are safe when they really aren't. The best way to tell if an offender is ready to live with children is to determine that he has successfully completed a treatment program that conforms to the highest treatment standards. In the field of sex offender treatment, those standards are set by the Association for the Treatment of Sexual Abusers (ATSA). If your partner is in a treatment program that does not conform to ATSA standards, he may not be fully benefiting from therapy. Inquire as to what other programs may be available locally that do meet ATSA standards. Remember, however, that completion of any treatment program does not guarantee that sex abusers won't offend again. It simply means that they have learned strategies and techniques that will help them manage their behavior if they choose not to reoffend.

In treatment, the sex offender learns first to be fully responsible for his abusive behaviors and stop blaming the victim, society, his partner, or intoxicants for his offense. He acknowledges that he alone is to blame for what he has done and that he alone must make sure it never happens again. He doesn't deny the possibility of future abuse and agrees that safety precautions and restrictions are necessary. If your partner continues to blame anyone or anything but himself, insists that it could never happen again, or resists the idea of safety planning, he has simply not learned the things he needs to know to live safely in a family.

In treatment, your partner should also have learned about the harm sexual abuse has caused to his victims. He should know the many ways in which sexual abuse hurts children and be able to imagine the feelings that abused children experience. He should also recognize the many ways abuse can affect the future life of a victim. His empathy for his victims should give him a powerful incentive to avoid harming others in the future.

The successfully treated offender has looked over his entire life and has developed insight into the various factors that may have contributed to his choice to abuse a child. He doesn't use these factors as excuses for his behavior but rather as ways of understanding what his emotional needs are and how he can begin to get those needs met in appropriate, nondestructive ways.

The offender who has successfully completed a qualified treatment program has a *relapse prevention plan*. He has examined his offense patterns. He understands how life events and his own thoughts, feelings, and behaviors have led him to sexually abuse in the past. By thoroughly exploring his behavior patterns, he has learned the types of situations, feelings, and thoughts that put him at risk for reoffending. He has developed strategies for coping with these high-risk factors through managing them or simply avoiding them. He has also learned some behavior modification techniques for reducing deviant sexual arousal and uses them consistently to make sex with a child less exciting.

In treatment, men learn how to have healthy relationships with other adults. They learn to communicate more effectively, solve problems by cooperating with others, and resolve conflicts in productive, nonviolent ways. They also develop ways of creating meaningful intimate relationships with other adults so that they are less likely to turn to children for closeness and affection.

Most important, the sex offender who has completed treatment knows that he is not cured. He knows that he might reoffend unless he remains constantly aware of his need to control his behavior. He doesn't fool himself by believing it's all in the past or that he's over his problem. And if you suggest that he is, he will correct you and gently remind you that he needs your acceptance of his lifelong problem in order to stay safe.

Any child living in a home with a known child abuser should be considered at risk for child sexual abuse. Taking precautions and developing restrictions, however, can help create a safer environment. Your participation in this process is crucial to the protection of your children. You are not expected to control the offender's behavior, but you are expected to maintain a home that manages your partner's known risk factors. Your role will be to supervise the contact between the offender and the children, enforce the safety rules, and take notice of any circumstances that could increase the risk of abuse.

Your Safety Plan

Your safety plan will include the following:

Prevention Strategies: These are rules family members will follow to promote healthy sexual boundaries and avoid high-risk factors for the offender. Although you cannot really control your partner's behavior, you and your family can make a commitment to understanding and managing risk factors that could trigger deviant thoughts in your partner.

Intervention Strategies: This is a plan you will adhere to if prevention strategies are failing, if sexual abuse seems likely despite prevention efforts, or if sexual abuse recurs. The plan should be specific and should detail exactly the steps you will take.

Prevention Strategies

Prevention of sexual abuse, especially when children are living in a home with an offender, requires careful planning. Your family should establish clear rules of behavior that everyone must follow.

Some examples of family rules:

The offender will not be alone or unsupervised with children at any time; any contact with children should be within the eyesight of an adult chaperone who is fully aware of the offender's history and accepts the potential for future abuse.

Family members will not bathe or shower together.

Family members (including children) will not share beds (excluding adult partners sleeping together).

The offender will not baby-sit any children.

The offender will not change children's diapers.

The offender will not dress or undress children.

The offender will not bathe children.

The offender will not discuss sex or dating with the children.

Physical affection between offender and children should be brief and should avoid bodily contact.

No tickling or wrestling is to take place between offender and children.

The offender will not have secrets with any child.

The offender will not swim with children.

The offender will never enter the bathroom while a child is in it nor will offender allow a child to enter the bathroom while he is in it.

No family member shall enter a bathroom or bedroom without knocking and receiving permission to enter.

All family members will be dressed at all times (pajamas or robes are OK if covering adequately).

No pornography (magazines, pictures, or videos) is allowed in the home.

The offender and nonoffending parent will not use alcohol or other drugs any time children are present (any intoxicant lowers inhibitions and impairs judgment). If alcohol or drugs played any role in his previous offending, the offender will not use drugs or alcohol at all.

If an offender has a diagnosed emotional disorder that requires medication, he will keep all scheduled appointments with his psychiatrist and take his medications according to the prescribed schedule.

These rules are only examples. You can use these rules as a starting point, but you will also have to design rules that specifically address your partner's grooming and offense patterns. Your safety plan must protect your particular family.

Real safety planning involves making some real sacrifices. To whatever extent possible, of course, the burden of the sacrifice should be placed on the offender, *not* on the children. In many families, for example, it is simply unsafe for the children to have friends sleep over while the offender is in the home. To not deprive the children of normal social relationships, the offender should make arrangements to sleep elsewhere rather than disallowing sleepovers. Some families find that they can't go to the beach together because seeing children in bathing suits might excite the offender; there is no reason, however, why the mother and children could not go to the beach. There will still be some times, though, when other family members will necessarily be inconvenienced. Because offenders should never be left alone with children, for example, when the wife goes anywhere, she will have to take the kids or hire a babysitter and have the offender leave, too.

Some families find it hard to accept that they must live differently from other families. It doesn't seem fair, they say. These sacrifices seem extreme. But families who want to stay together eventually come to accept that staying together safely takes work. Safety doesn't just happen because you want it to. Long-term safety takes ongoing commitment to living a lifestyle that protects children from potential abuse. In the long run, the sacrifices are a small price to pay for the safety of your children and the freedom of your partner.

If your partner had a drinking problem and was in recovery from alcoholism, you would probably do everything you could to support him. You might even give up drinking yourself, even if you liked an occasional glass of wine, because you wouldn't want to tempt him to drink. His recovery would be more important to you than that glass of wine. When friends were invited to dinner and offered to bring beer, you would ask them to bring dessert instead. You would help your partner create a lifestyle that eliminated any situations that would put him at risk for drinking, right?

By supporting your partner in his relapse prevention plan, you will be helping him to avoid molesting another child. The family safety rules are designed to create an environment that minimizes the likelihood of his developing abusive thoughts or urges and restricts his opportunities for acting on any such thoughts.

Writing Out Your Partner's
Relapse Prevention Strategies

If you are living with an offender who has successfully completed treatment, you should be familiar with his relapse prevention plan. A relapse prevention plan is a set of rules that your partner has designed in treatment specifically to address his risk factors. Risk factors include any people, situations, thoughts, or feelings that give him the urge to sexually abuse a child. The relapse prevention plan outlines situations to avoid, ways to escape risky situations, and specific coping strategies to control his behavior. Your family rules should include rules for the offender to follow that are specifically related to his relapse prevention plan.

TABLE 8.1 Relapse Prevention Plan Work Sheet

Internal	
Thoughts	*Feelings*

External			
Places	*Situations, Events*	*Stimuli*	*Grooming*

Discuss with your partner his relapse prevention plan. Refer back to Table 6.1. Together, using the blank Table 8.1, write down each of his strategies for avoiding, escaping, or managing all of the factors.

Intervention Strategies

Intervention strategies are steps you will take to protect your children if you see the offender you live with straying from his relapse prevention plan *or* if sexual abuse occurs by your partner or anyone else. If your partner seems not to be following his prevention plan or the safety plan your family has agreed on, he is at risk for abusing a child. You will be helping him by making it clear that unless he follows the rules strictly, he and your children cannot live together.

Your intervention plan must include a strategy to separate the child from the offender *immediately* in a high-risk situation. Prepare at least three options regarding how you can separate the child from the offender, if necessary. If prevention strategies are not working, it will be safe for the offender and child to be reunited *only* after the offender has demonstrated a commitment to family safety rules and his relapse prevention plan. The offender should also return to treatment with his therapist to address his straying from agreed-on rules.

Some possible intervention options:

Taking the child with you to a hotel

Asking the offender to leave your home and securing a restraining order through the court or changing the locks

Going with the child to live with a trusted friend or relative until the situation is resolved

> Your child needs to know you believe her, that you will protect her, and that you are on her side. Your loyalty should be with your child, not with the offender.

If you believe sexual abuse has occurred (with any perpetrator), you must *immediately*

Separate the child from the offender

Contact your local child protection agency and report the incident to the authorities

Cooperate with the child welfare workers and law enforcement officials conducting an investigation

> Remember, you are not protecting anyone by protecting the abuser. For everyone to stay safe, the offender needs to return to treatment and separate himself from children. Usually, an offender will not choose to do these things on his own, and the only way he will get help is if the authorities force him to. Your children and the children of others need your protection much more than the offender does!

Anticipating Difficulties in Implementing Your Plan

Your plan sounds good now. You are committed to following it. It will involve sacrifices, but you're willing to do it and so is your partner.

But what will happen 6 months or a few years from now? You see your partner straying from the plan, you notice that the whole family has gotten a little lax about the rules. You hesitate to say anything because everything seems to be going so well, but you decide to talk to your partner about it. He acts hurt and says,

> Oh honey, we don't really need those rules anymore, do we? We did the plan to satisfy the counselor, but we know that nothing will happen. You trust me, don't you? You love me, don't you? It'll be OK. I just want to live like a normal family.

How do you think you will feel if this happens? Probably, you will feel guilty for mentioning the plan. You won't want to hurt your partner. You will want to believe that everything can be OK. You may have a teeny little nagging doubt, but your doubt will quickly be replaced by guilt for even thinking such a thing about the man you love.

What if your partner has been violent with you in the past? What if he is a very controlling and intimidating force around the house? Will you feel comfortable even mentioning the plan in the first place? Or will you be afraid to?

What if you are dependent on your partner emotionally or financially (or both)? Will you really be prepared to enforce intervention plans? Do you believe that you can support yourself independently? If necessary, will you leave him? Or kick him out?

Think honestly about all of these considerations before you make a decision to reconcile with your partner. You must be sure that you are prepared to protect your children from the sexual abuser in your home.

Family Therapy Sessions to Educate Everyone and Put the Plan in Place

After your *Connections* group meetings are completed, there will still be important work to be done. If you are planning to live with a sex offender who did not abuse one of the children in your family, you will be required to attend at least six family therapy sessions (more if your therapist thinks it appropriate). You will spend two sessions with your partner learning more about his offense patterns, grooming behaviors, and relapse prevention plans. Your children will attend a sexual abuse prevention session with the therapist. Your whole family will meet at least once, and at that session your partner will tell the children (using age-appropriate language) what he has done and why your family will need to live differently from other families, with special rules. Then, you and your partner will finalize your family safety plan, present and explain the plan to the children, and sign the plan with your therapist.

If the offender's victim will be living in your home, your family will go through some special additional family therapy, called the "clarification process." This process will be discussed in detail in the next chapter.

WORK SHEET #8: FAMILY SAFETY PLAN

Family Safety Contract

The _____ Family agrees to the following rules designed for child safety during visitation and after reunification.

Prevention

1. The offender will not be alone or unsupervised with children at any time; any contact with children will be within the eyesight of an adult chaperone who is fully aware of the offender's history and accepts the potential for future abuse to occur.

2. The following people are approved to supervise contact between the offender and children:

_____

_____

_____

3. When the nonoffending parent leaves the room, offender will

_____

_____

_____

4. Our child care plans for work:

_____

_____

_____

5. Offender will never be responsible for babysitting or supervising children.

6. Discipline of the children will be done primarily by the nonoffending caretaker.

7. Offender will not discuss sex or dating with the children.

8. Physical affection between offender and children will be brief and will avoid bodily contact.

9. Physical hygiene assistance is always to be done by the nonoffending caretaker. This includes

    Bathing

    Dressing

    Diapering

    Toileting

10. There will be no tickling or wrestling between offender and children.

11. Offender will not have secrets with any child.

12. Offender will never enter the children's bedrooms alone.

13. Offender will never enter the bathroom while a child is in it nor will offender allow a child to enter the bathroom while he is in it.

14. All bedroom and bathroom doors will have locks.

15. If mutually agreed, children will be permitted to lock doors.

16. All family members will sleep in their own beds.

17. All family members bathe, shower, and toilet separately.

18. No family member shall enter a bathroom or bedroom without knocking and receiving permission to enter.

19. All family members will be dressed at all times (pajamas or robes are OK if covering adequately).

20. Alcohol and drug use is completely and strictly prohibited if substance use was in any way involved in previous sex offenses.

21. For offenders who have not used alcohol or drugs in previous offenses, rules for moderate use will be established.

22. No pornography or sexually oriented materials (magazines, pictures, or videos) will in the home.

Intervention

In the event that prevention measures break down and offender does not appear to be following the specified rules, the nonoffending caretaker will immediately

Separate offender and children by

1. _____

2. _____

3. _____

In the event that child sexual abuse recurs, the nonoffending caretaker will immediately

- Report the abuse to the local child protection agency

  _____

- Cooperate with authorities conducting an investigation

  _____

- Secure a restraining order

  _____

-

  _____

-

  _____

Some other, more specific rules that apply to our family based on the abuser's past patterns, grooming behaviors, and known high-risk factors:

_____

_____

_____

_____

_____

_____

_____

_____

CHAPTER
9

Considering Reunification With an Offender and His Victim

The Clarification Process

Selby and Livingston[1] presented a model of clarification for families preparing for visitation and reunification. This chapter is adapted from their model.

Even more complicated than having a sex offender live in a home with nonvictimized children is the situation in which an abuser is planning to live in the home with one or more of his victims. *Much of the time, this situation will not be workable and should not be attempted.* You have learned about the impact of sexual abuse and the many ways that victims are traumatized by their abuse experiences. Nothing could be more unfair to a victim of sexual abuse than to be reexposed against her will to the same situation that has already hurt her so deeply. If bringing the abuser back into the home with the victim is to be contemplated, the victim must fully approve of the move and no possibility of revictimizing that child can be allowed.

Before such a reunification can be contemplated, the victim must have received adequate therapy to address the sexual abuse and her therapist must agree that the move is emotionally safe for her. The offender must have successfully completed a sex offender treatment program that fully complies with ATSA standards. In addition, he will need to pass a maintenance or monitoring polygraph to ensure that he has been following the recommendations of his treatment program and avoiding deviant fantasizing or acting out. Nonabused siblings will be involved in the clarification process as well. You must complete *Connections*.

If these conditions have been met, the reunification process can be attempted, but it must be kept in mind that the victim can change her mind at any time, and *her needs must always take first priority over the offender's needs*. If they do not, everyone in the family, including the offender, will know that you are not willing to protect your children at the risk of losing the offender. There will be no safety for any of the children in such a family.

Before reunification can begin, important issues must be addressed, and additional therapy sessions will be needed. These sessions are called *clarification sessions*. The clarification process is essential for the victim, as it involves the offender acknowledging to the victim (and the other children in the home) that he alone was responsible for the sexual abuse and the resulting legal consequences. He will also acknowledge his manipulation of all the family members and his betrayal of the family's trust. Nonabused siblings will be involved in the clarification process as well.

The goals of clarification are several. Most important, the victim is absolved of any and all responsibility. All family members are helped to see themselves as victims of the offender's behavior, his manipulation, and his deceit. The other children in the home will be made aware of the offender's grooming patterns. The potential risk for future abuse will be emphasized, as will the need for safety planning. The children will also be made aware of the ways in which the offender alienated them from each other and pitted them against each other as a way of isolating the victim, making her more needy and therefore more vulnerable to his abuse. The child protective services and criminal court systems, instead of being portrayed as enemies of the family, will be recognized as vital in the protection of the children. Last, the victim will be seen as the hero she was for speaking out and providing the family with the opportunity for change and recovery.

The clarification process takes time and preparation, and several therapy sessions are necessary to complete it. The first step is the victim's statement that she is willing and ready to begin. If all therapists involved (with the child victim's therapist taking the lead) agree that your family is ready for clarification and reunification, the following five steps will then take place:

1. The victim (with help from her therapist if needed) will write a letter to the offender, which will be delivered through the victim's therapist to the offender's therapist. The letter will give the child an opportunity to discuss how she felt during the abuse, what the disclosure process was like, the ways in which the abuse has changed her life, and her current feelings about beginning family therapy. It is important for the victim to spend as much time as needed drafting the letter, discussing it with her therapist, and revising it if necessary.

2. Based on his understanding of the victim's needs after reading her letter, the offender (with feedback from his therapist and treatment group) will write a clarification letter outlining his sole responsibility for the abuse and

all of its consequences. He will describe how he manipulated the victim and the whole family and alienated the victim from the family. He will validate the victim's feelings, meaning he will recognize them as real and important and deserving of the utmost respect. Last, he will clearly and completely release the victim from responsibility for the abuse and specifically state that she did the right thing by disclosing.

3. The victim will review the offender's letter with her therapist and have a chance to respond again in writing if needed. If the victim is ready to begin face-to-face meetings, the sessions will be arranged. The victim's therapist should be present for support in the initial family therapy session, even if the mother's therapist or offender's therapist is actually facilitating the session.

4. Several sessions may be needed to achieve the goals just described. Sibling issues will be specifically addressed (see discussion to follow).

5. Because she is most knowledgeable of the offender's abuse patterns, the victim will play a central role (if she chooses) in developing family rules for the safety plan.

Sibling Issues

Siblings of the victim also suffered when the sexual abuse took place, even if they were unaware of it. Sometimes, siblings resent the child victim because she seemed to be the "favorite" and received special treatment from the offender. This special treatment, as you now know, was actually the offender grooming her for the abuse, but the other children may not be able to understand the distinction. Siblings might also resent the victim for telling and "breaking up the family." Often offenders try to convince nonabused siblings that the victim is lying, and not infrequently, they succeed. Looking back, you may now realize that you might have even given the message to the other children that you doubted the word of the victim and didn't know who to believe.

Sometimes sexual abuse victims are placed in foster care while their nonabused siblings remain at home, often with the abuser. This occurs most often when the victim is a girl and the other siblings are boys. (Sometimes child welfare workers and courts mistakenly believe that children of the opposite gender of the victim are not at risk. What we know, primarily through polygraphing, is that some offenders molest children of both sexes). All the time that the victim is out of the home and the offender is in the home—especially if he is denying the offenses or blaming the victim—is time that the siblings are continuing to be alienated from the victim. Their feelings toward her are being poisoned by the offender.

By the time the victim is finally returned to the home, her relationships with her brothers and sisters may be severely damaged. It is critical that the clarification sessions address this damage directly and begin the reparation process. The siblings must fully understand how they have been manipulated and lied to by the offender: how he intentionally singled out the victim and groomed her, how he set her up for abuse, how he trapped her into not exposing the abuse, how he called her a liar when she exposed the abuse, how he led everyone to blame her for the misery and suffering he brought on the family. All of the bad feelings the offender has led the siblings to have for the victim only compound the victim's suffering. She needs and deserves the support and understanding of her siblings more than ever as she comes back into the family.

Note

1. Selby, T., & Livingston, M. (1999, September). *Family Reunification Decision in Parent-Child Molest Cases.* Paper presented at the 18th Annual Research and Treatment Conference of the Association for the Treatment of Sexual Abusers, Orlando, Florida.

CHAPTER
10

Making Sense of It All

Now that you have learned all about sexual abuse, you will have the opportunity to practice some of what you know. You will begin by reading a story about a family who has experienced child sexual abuse. Then you will be given some questions to answer about how to make the family safer. (All names in the following story are fictitious, and any resemblance to any actual persons, living or dead, is purely coincidental.)

The Smith Family

Jan and Fred Smith had been married for 3 years. Jan had a 7-year-old daughter, Erica, from her first marriage. The Smiths seemed to everyone to be the "perfect family." Fred spent a lot of time with Erica, helping her to draw, paint, and read. He coached her soccer team and most weekends could be seen in the yard kicking the ball around with her. He often took Erica out for ice cream or to the movies, and Jan always appreciated this help because it meant having some time to herself. Jan was proud of her family and happy that Erica had adjusted so well to the new marriage.

One day, following a sexual abuse awareness program at school, Erica disclosed to her teacher that her stepfather had touched her "privacy" on two occasions. The first time, she said, was in the car on the way home from the movies. She stated that he began rubbing her thigh and then rubbed the inside of her leg and tried to put his hand inside her shorts. The second time, they were lying together on the couch watching TV when Fred rubbed Erica's back and buttocks and slipped his hand around the front, rubbing her crotch.

Erica's teacher was concerned and called child protective services. Jan was shocked when social workers and the police arrived at her house and explained what Erica had said. Jan was sure it was all a mistake, pointing out how close Fred and Erica were. Social workers took Erica for a medical exam, but the doctor found no evidence of sexual abuse. During the exam, when the doctor asked Erica if her stepfather had touched her in a bad way, she said that she had made a mistake and that nothing had really happened. When Fred was questioned, he denied abusing Erica. He explained that he did show her where her private parts were and tell her that no one could touch her there. He stated that she must have been confused during the sexual abuse awareness program and that the teacher may have misunderstood Erica's statements.

The case was closed, and Jan was relieved. She loved her husband and loved her daughter and couldn't believe something like this could happen in her family. Besides, she never saw any inappropriate behavior on the part of her husband. She told herself that she would watch the two of them closely and if anything were to happen, she would handle it herself.

Things settled down at home, and Erica seemed happy. A few months later, she developed a urinary tract infection. Jan took Erica to the doctor, and he prescribed an antibiotic. It seemed to Jan that right around this time, Erica began to change. Suddenly, she woke up with nightmares in the middle of the night. Fred would go in to console her, and Jan went back to sleep. Fred always did a good job of calming Erica down.

Sometimes, Erica would wet her bed. It also seemed that she was very clingy lately, not wanting Jan to leave her at home with Fred and crying at the door as she would leave.

Jan figured that Erica was just going through a difficult phase. She was shocked when, 8 months after the first allegation, social workers and police showed up at her door again. They stated that there had been an incident at school. Erica had told a little boy that she would suck on his penis if he would buy her some ice cream at lunch. When the guidance counselor took Erica into her office to talk about what had happened, Erica told her that her daddy puts his penis in her mouth and kisses her peepee.

Jan was distraught. She told herself that the boy must have initiated this incident and that the guidance counselor was putting words in Erica's mouth. She said that she had never seen anything unusual between her husband and daughter. Social workers took Erica to a foster home, stating that Jan had failed to protect Erica from sexual abuse.

Erica felt that she was being punished because she was sent away from her home. She was afraid she would never see her parents again, and she missed her mother. She also missed her school and her friends. She felt that her mother blamed her for upsetting the family, although she didn't quite understand what she had done wrong.

When Jan visited Erica at the foster home, she could see how lonely and scared Erica was. At this point, Jan began to understand that she must take action. She asked Fred to leave the home until the matter could be resolved. He moved out the next day, and the following week, Erica was returned home to Jan's custody under a protective services order.

Fred ended up confessing to sexual abuse with Erica, but claimed that Erica liked it and would have said "no" if she didn't want to do it. He also blamed Jan for not having sex with him more frequently and not liking to perform oral sex. He was convinced that because he hadn't used physical force, he had not hurt Erica.

Jan, in therapy with Erica, learned that the abuse had continued after the first disclosure. After the first investigation, Fred could see that no one would believe a child, and Erica became convinced that Jan didn't want to know what was going on. Erica said that Fred had told her that this was their secret game and their special activity. He explained that other people might not understand how special they were to each other and might think it was wrong. He told Erica that Mommy would get mad if she knew. Erica knew that Mommy would get mad at her because she had been told in school about "bad touching" and believed that because she liked Daddy's special attention, she was bad, too.

After 6 months of therapy, Erica seemed to be doing OK. She was a very active child, and she was getting straight As in school and excelling at sports. Jan dropped out of therapy, convinced that Erica was fine and that the abuse seemed not to have affected her.

Fred pleaded no contest to reduced charges and was sentenced to 18 months in prison. He is attending a parenting class while in prison so that he could learn to be a better parent to Erica when he gets out. He feels relieved because he has received letters from Erica reassuring him that she doesn't blame him for anything. She also says she is doing well in school, so he knows she wasn't really harmed by what happened, no matter what the social workers say. He knows that he will never abuse a child again because he has learned his lesson.

Erica believes that she was responsible for sending Fred to jail. She feels guilty and sad because she loves Fred and misses him. She doesn't like to talk about the abuse in therapy. She participates in a lot of activities to keep busy so she doesn't have to think about Fred being in prison or how sad her mom is.

Jan feels stressed out, lonely, and guilty. She is behind on her bills because Fred made a lot more money than she. She misses Fred although she is angry at him. She wants to stay together and work things out when he is released from prison.

WORK SHEET #10

After reading the case scenario, answer the following questions. You must be able to demonstrate that you can apply the concepts you learned in group and in your workbook.

1. Name three (3) activities that occurred between Fred and Erica that are defined as child sexual abuse.

_____

_____

_____

_____

2. Give two (2) reasons why Erica might have recanted the first allegation of sexual abuse.

_____

_____

_____

_____

3. List three (3) emotional signs of abuse that Erica displayed.

_____

_____

_____

_____

4. List three (3) behavioral signs of abuse that Erica displayed.

_____

_____

_____

_____

5. List a physical (medical) sign that Erica was being abused.

_____

_____

_____

_____

6. Describe why a medical exam revealing no physical evidence of sexual abuse does not mean that abuse did not occur.

_____

_____

_____

_____

7. Describe three (3) characteristics of an incestuous offender.

_____

_____

_____

_____

8. Name three (3) grooming behaviors that Fred engaged in with Erica.

_____

_____

_____

_____

9. Describe five (5) feelings that Erica may have had during and after the sexual abuse.

_____

_____

_____

_____

10. Describe three (3) factors that might affect the impact of the sexual abuse on Erica and why.

_____

_____

_____

11. Explain three (3) reasons why Jan might have denied that the abuse occurred.

_____

_____

_____

12. Name and describe five (5) things this family must do before re-unification should occur.

_____

_____

_____

_____

13. Name and describe three (3) things this family can do after reuni-fying that will help promote child safety.

_____

_____

_____

Fill in the following chart by giving an example of how each Smith family member displayed each type of denial. You may quote a statement that the family member might have made or describe their thought or actions.

Type of Denial	Offender	Nonoffending Parent	Child
Denial of the facts			
Denial of awareness			
Denial of responsibility			
Denial of impact			
Denial of the need for treatment			

TABLE 10.1 *Connections* Safety Checklist

✔ = The safety objective has been achieved, as demonstrated by your behaviors, statements, or situation.

X = The safety objective has *not* been achieved; you do not demonstrate the behavior or the situation does not exist.

N/A = The safety objective does not apply to your family.

Description of Safety Objective	Complete
1. Caretaker and offender both acknowledge that abuse occurred and that it was not the child's fault.	
2. Caretaker acknowledges and describes her responsibility to manage risk factors in the home.	
3. Caretaker acknowledges the offender's potential for future abuse.	
4. Caretaker can name the five types of denial.	
5. Caretaker can give original examples of the five types of denial.	
6. Caretaker can spontaneously recognize denial in self, offender, and others.	
7. Caretaker can describe common feelings of sexually abused children.	
8. Caretaker can accurately describe her own child's feelings.	
9. Caretaker can accurately describe the impact of sexual abuse on her child(ren) or can speculate about her partner's victim.	
10. Caretaker demonstrates empathy toward her child(ren) or her partner's victim(s).	
11. Caretaker can name and describe at least five physical symptoms of child sexual abuse.	
12. Caretaker can name and describe at least five behavioral symptoms of child sexual abuse.	
13. Caretaker can name and describe at least five emotional symptoms of child sexual abuse.	
14. Caretaker can, in retrospect, name at least five symptoms her child exhibited while being sexually abused.	
15. Caretaker can identify signs to look for in the future, and can propose interventions if needed.	
16. Caretaker demonstrates effective management of child behavior problems resulting from sexual abuse, including sexually reactive behavior.	
17. If applicable, caretaker can discuss her own childhood abuse and its impact on her reaction to her own child's abuse.	

18. Caretaker can name at least six grooming behaviors offenders may use.	
19. Caretaker can describe and give examples of grooming behaviors, offense patterns, and relapse prevention strategies.	
20. Caretaker can describe her partner's offense pattern, grooming behaviors, high-risk situations, thoughts, feelings, and behaviors.	
21. Caretaker can describe in detail her partner's relapse prevention plan and demonstrates behaviors that support her partner in his relapse prevention plan.	
22. Caretaker can name at least five strategies for protecting children from sexual abuse.	
23. Caretaker has developed and implemented prevention strategies with her own children.	
24. Offender has successfully completed a sex offender rehabilitation program or is enrolled in and participating actively in a sex offender treatment program.	
25. Offender demonstrates understanding of his offense patterns and has developed and implemented a realistic relapse prevention plan.	
26. Victim or other children express a desire to be reunited with caretaker or offender or both, and this is supported by child(ren)'s therapist.	
27. Children have knowledge of offender's past sexually abusive behavior.	
28. Children demonstrate knowledge of prevention education.	
29. Caretaker can financially support herself and the children independently.	
30. There is no evidence of current substance abuse by either adult.	
31. There is no history of domestic violence.	
32. Family safety plan includes prevention and intervention strategies.	
33. All family members have agreed to and signed the safety plan.	

This checklist reflects my assessment of the safety indicators in the _____ family.

_____

Connections Therapist   Date

I have reviewed my therapist's safety assessment checklist.

_____

Client   Date

TABLE 10.2 *Connections* Attendance Checklist

Description of Session	Date
Initial intake assessment	
Educational Group 1: Introductions and program description	
Educational Group 2: Common feelings of parents and partners	
Support group	
Educational Group 3: Denial in family members	
Support group	
Educational Group 4: How sexual abuse affects children and families	
Support group	
Educational Group 5: Signs and symptoms of sexual abuse in children	
Support group	
Educational Group 6: What if you were sexually abused as a child?	
Support group	
Educational Group 7: Learning about sexual offenders	
Support group	
Educational Group 8: How to protect your children from sexual abuse	
Support group	
Educational Group 9: Developing a safety plan for your family	
Educational Group 10: Review of safety plans	
Support group and closing discussion	
Partners' session: Reviewing the offender's cycle	
Partners' session: Reviewing the offender's relapse prevention plan	
Family session: Child sexual abuse prevention education	
Family session: Offender disclosure and validation of responsibility	
Partners' session: Detailing the family safety plan	
Family session: Reviewing and signing the family safety plan	

About the Authors

Jill S. Levenson, MSW, is a licensed clinical social worker and a full-time faculty member at Florida International University (FIU) School of Social Work. She earned her master's degree in Social Work at the University of Maryland in 1987 and has worked in the child welfare field since 1985. Beginning her career as an investigator of child abuse and neglect cases, she has since worked in several community agencies treating abused children, perpetrators, adult survivors, and nonoffending parents. From 1994 through 1999, she served on the faculty at FIU's Professional Development Center, where she provided training and consultation for the Florida Department of Children and Families. In her private practice, she provides evaluation and treatment for sexual offenders and nonoffending parents and provides consultation and expert witness testimony on the topic of child sexual abuse. She is a member of the National Association of Social Workers, the American Professional Society on the Abuse of Children, and the Association for the Treatment of Sexual Abusers (ATSA). She sits on the Board of Directors of ATSA's Florida chapter. She has presented locally and internationally on the treatment of sexual offenders and their partners.

John W. Morin, PhD, is a licensed psychologist who earned his doctorate from the University of Miami. He has specialized in sexual deviance for the past 8 years in both community and institutional settings. In 1991, he became the director of the sexual offender program at an outpatient mental health center and in 1994 founded the Center for Offender Rehabilitation and Education in Fort Lauderdale. As a contracted consultant and treatment provider for both the Florida Department of Corrections and the Florida Department of Children and Families, he specializes in the evaluation of sexually violent predators. He has lectured locally and nationally on the management of sex offenders. He is a member of the American Psychological Association and ATSA and sits on the Board of Directors of the Florida chapter of ATSA.

The authors have also published *The Road to Freedom,* a comprehensive, competency-based program for sexual offenders in treatment.